世 界 文 化 遗 产　Heritage Site of Cultural Anthropology

登 攀 长 城 证 明 书

Certificate to show that you have climbed the Great Wall of China

不 到 長 城 非 好 漢

NOT A PLUCKY HERO UNTIL ONE REACHES THE GREAT WALL

_____　　登攀万里长城，特此证明。

This is to certify that _____ has climbed

the Simatai Great Wall of China.

日期(Date)：_____

图书在版编目（CIP）数据

司马台长城／杨涛，旅舜编．—北京：中国民族摄影
艺术出版社，2005.12
ISBN 7-80069-701-0

Ⅰ.司... Ⅱ.①杨...②旅... Ⅲ.长城－画册
Ⅳ.K928.77-64

中国版本图书馆CIP数据核字（2005）第124775号

策　　划：旅　舜

责任编辑：鲁宝春

执行编辑：李　江

摄　　影：吴健骅　张肇基　王文波

　　　　　谭　明　杨　茵　李　江

　　　　　赵鸿生　武冀平　刘思敏

设　　计：赵鸿生

中国民族摄影艺术出版社　出版

开本：787×1092毫米　　1/12

印张：8　印数：5000册

2005年11月第1版　第1次印刷

司马台长城

SIMATAI GREAT WALL

司馬台長城

사마대장성

DIE GROßE MAUER BEI SIMATAI

LA GRANDE MURAILLE DE SIMATAI

LA GRANDE MURAGLIA DI SIMATAI

LA GRAN MURALLA EN SIMATAI

司马台望京楼
The Beijing-Watching Tower on the Simatai Great Wall.
司馬台の望京楼
사마대 망경루
Der Wangjing-Wachtturm der Großen Mauer bei Simatai
La tour de guet Ayant vue sur Beijing.
Simatai: la Torre d'osservazione su Beijing
Torre del Mirador de Beijing

司马台望京楼
The Beijing-Watching Tower on the Simatai Great Wall.
司馬台の望京楼
사마대 망경루
Der Wangjing-Wachtturm der Großen Mauer bei Simatai
La tour de guet Ayant vue sur Beijing.
Simatai: la Torre d'osservazione su Beijing
Torre del Mirador de Beijing

司马台仙女楼
The Fairy Tower on the Simatai Great Wall.
司馬台の仙女楼
사마대 선녀루
Der Xiannü-Wachtturm der Großen Mauer bei Simatai
La tour de guet de la Fée.
Simatai: la Torre della Fata
Torre de Hada

司马台长城

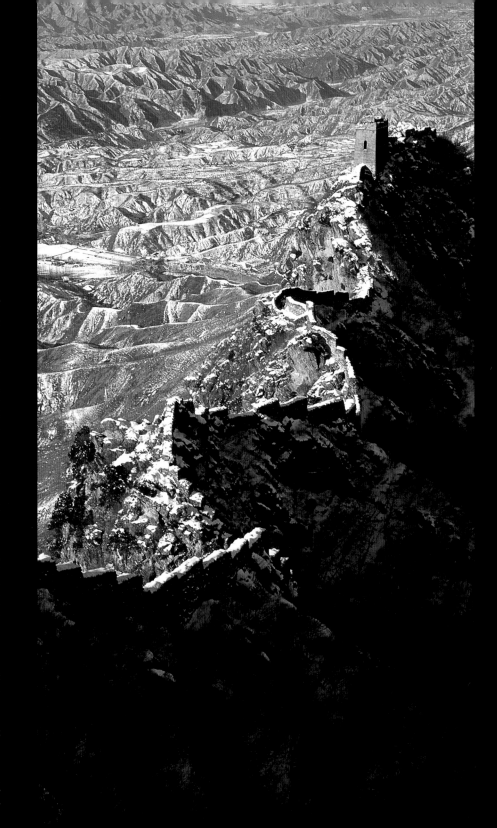

司马台长城位于北京东北部120千米的险关重镇古北口境内，始建于明洪武初年（1368年），是至今保留最完整的一段明长城。司马台长城全长5.4千米，有敌楼35座。整段长城构思精巧、设计奇特、形态各异，它集万里长城众多特色于一地，形成了一段"奇妙的长城"，且有"长城博物馆"之称。

司马台长城沿刀削斧劈似的山脊修筑，蜿蜒曲折，惊险无比，尤其是天梯和天桥两段。天梯是单面墙长城，坡陡墙窄，最窄处不足半米，呈直梯状沿山体上升，两侧是陡峭悬崖，俯首下望，令人瞠目结舌。天梯顶端便是天桥，长不过百米，只有一块砖那么宽，约40厘米左右，两侧的悬崖绝壁更是令人不寒而栗，到这里的人们都说："过天桥难，难于上青天"，这里是明长城中最险要的地段之一，也是最惊险刺激的地方。

司马台长城的敌楼和城墙建筑形式奇特多样，最大的一个特点是敌楼密集，两楼相距最近仅43.8米，最远600米，而其他地方的长城一般都在100米－200米之间。若按明代修筑长城的规定，每500米修敌楼一座，此段长城应该说是一个例外。从外观来看，敌楼有单眼楼、双眼楼、三眼楼、四眼楼和五眼楼，有单层楼，上下相通的双层楼和三层楼。它们均为空心敌楼，大小不一、形态各异，是按驻军的官衔等级、驻防人数以及地势险要程度分别建造的。从内部结构来看，有砖结构、砖木结构、砖石结构；又有单室、双室、多室之分；房间布局有"田"字、"井"字；楼顶形制多样，有平顶、穹窿顶、八角藻井顶、覆斗顶；就连门窗也新颖别致，有边门、中间门、有砖券和石券，还有技艺精湛的雕花花岗岩石门。这些在万里长城中较为罕见，也是吸引游人驻足的亮点。

司马台长城虽以山势险峻雄奇为主景，但长城角下的鸳鸯湖却赋予了这段长城以灵性，清澈的湖水造就了一派碧波荡漾、湖光帆影的宁静景致。鸳鸯湖是由冷泉和温泉汇聚而成的，湖水冷暖各半，从不结冰。在炎热的夏季，到这里荡舟湖上，让人暑气顿消，神清气爽。

司马台长城不仅有绮丽的风光，更是一座研究长城历史文化遗产的宝库。近年来，这段长城上发现了许多文物。如石刻"题名碑"，碑上记载着当年修建长城时的情况，以及与建城有关的官员的名字，同时在几处城墙和敌楼上还发现带有戳印文字的砖石，上面刻有参加修建长城的军队名称和年代，如"万历五年山东左营造"、"万历五年宁夏营造"等字样。这种带有戳印文字的长城砖除了说明造砖的年代，标明监督的军营，还见证了当年建造长城的明确分工。同时发现的还有一批文物，有明代守城将士使用过的铁炮、石炮、铁镢铁铳、手雷、三眼铳、铁弹丸、火药勺等，还有士兵用过的生产生活用具，如锄头、铁铲、菜刀、铁灯碗等，这些文物为研究明代长城及明代历史提供了很有价值的实物资料。

著名长城专家罗哲文曾这样说道："中国长城是世界之最，而司马台长城是中国长城之最。" 长城是中国人民，也是全人类的文化遗产，司马台长城则无疑是这份宝贵遗产中光彩熠熠的一颗明珠。

由于司马台长城建在地势险要的山巅之上，为保证游客安全，管理部门规定从东12号敌楼向东禁止游客通行。游客已难以领略全段长城的奇绝风光，希望本画册精美的图片能为你弥补些许遗憾。

SIMATAI GREAT WALL

The Simatai section of the Great Wall is situated at Gubeikou, an old town of strategic significance, 120 kilometers northeast of urban Beijing. First built in 1368, the first year during the reign of Emperor Hongwu of the Ming Dynasty (1368-1644), it is among the best-preserved sections of the Great Wall of the Ming Dynasty. The Simatai section spans 5.4 kilometers and has a total of 35 watchtowers. A fantastic section characterized by delicate and unique design and diversified structures, it incorporates a variety of styles of other parts of the Great Wall and is thus reputed as the Museum of the Great Wall.

Zigzagging along steep mountain ranges, this section of the Great Wall features an unmatched peril, especially the two parts respectively called the Heavenly Stairway and the Heavenly Bridge. The Heavenly Stairway, in fact, is a narrow section with a single wall, whose narrowest part is less than half of a meter. The section mounts like a stairway along the mountainside. On both sides are steep and hazardous cliffs, and one would hold breath if he looked down. The Heavenly Bridge, 100 meters in length and some 40 centimeters in width, is situated on the top of the Heavenly Stairway. Cliffs on both sides of the Heavenly Bridge appears to be even more breathtaking. "It is hard to climb onto the Heavenly Bridge—even harder than mounting onto the sky," said some visitors. This part is among the most dangerous but extremely exciting sections of the Great Wall built during the Ming Dynasty.

The walls and watchtowers of the Simatai section of the Great Wall exhibit a unique design and varied architectural styles. One characteristic of this section is its densely-dispersed watchtowers, with the nearest distance of two watchtowers being 43.8 meters and the farthest distance 600 meters. Usually, the nearest distance between two watchtowers is 100-200 meters in other parts of the Great Wall. According to routines of the walls built during the Ming Dynasty, the interval between each two watchtower should be 500 meters. However, the Simatai section is an exception. In the terms of appearance, some watchtowers there have only a single window, and others have two, three, four or five windows; some are one-story structures, and there are also interconnected two- or three-story watchtowers. Various in size and appearance, they were constructed in light of the rank and amount of stationed troops, as well as geographical conditions. Some watchtowers are built with bricks, and others are brick-and-wooden structures or brick-and-stone structures. The watchtowers accommodate one or more chambers. Their roofs are different in design, such as plain roofs, hollow roofs, octagonal painted roofs and reserved-container-shaped roofs. Their gates and windows are also delicately designed, among which include side gates, central gates, brick arches, stone arches and even carved granite gates featuring superb craftsmanship. All of these make Simatai unique among other sections of the Great Wall, thus attracting numerous tourists to visit.

The Simatai section is mainly noted for its magnificent but perilous topography, and meanwhile the Mandarin Duck Lake at the foot of the Great Wall gives this section spirit. The reflections of boat sails on crystal-clear water add a serene and tranquil touch. The lake is where a hot spring and a cold spring meet, so half of its water is warm and the other half is cold. The water never gets frozen there. In scorching summer, boating on the lake is an ideal way to escape from summer heat and get refreshed.

Besides picturesque landscapes, this section of the Great Wall is also a treasure of historical and cultural heritages. In recent years, many historical relics have been unearthed there, including the Stele of Autographs. On the stele is inscribed with information about the construction of the Great Wall as well as the names of officials in charge of

司马台长城入口处
The entrance to the Simatai Great Wall.
司馬台長城の入口
사마대장성 입구
Eingang zur Großen Mauer bei Simatai.
Entrée de la Grande Muraille de Simatai.
Simatai: l'accesso alla Grande Muraglia
Entrada de la sección Simatai de la Gran Muralla

construction. On several walls and watchtowers are discovered many bricks and stones with official seals and inscriptions to record the names of troops constructing the Great Wall and the construction time, such as "Constructed by Shandong Left Battalion in the Fifth Year of Emperor Wanli's Reign" and "Constructed by Ningxia Battalion in the Fifth Year of Emperor Wanli's Reign." Besides recording the supervising army and construction time, these inscribed bricks have also witnessed explicit division of labor during the construction of the Great Wall. Among discovered relics also include iron cannons, stone cannons, iron arrowheads, iron guns, iron blunderbusses, grenades, tri-tube guns, iron bullets and powder scoops used troops stationed there, as well as such living appliances and tools as hoes, shovels, kitchen knives and iron lamp bowls. These relics are valuable materials to research the Ming-Dynasty Great Wall and the history of the dynasty.

"The Great Wall is unmatched around the world," said Luo Zhewen, a renowned specialist in research of the Great Wall. "And the Simatai section is unmatched among other sections of the Great Wall." The Great Wall is known as a rare cultural heritage of the Chinese nation and even the whole mankind, and the Simatai section is undoubtedly a brilliant pearl of the cultural heritage.

The Simatai section of the Great Wall is constructed on precipitous mountaintops. For the sake of tourists' safety, therefore, the administrative department of the scenic area has designated the part beyond the No.12 watchtower as a "no-entry zone." We hope this illustrated book will relieve your disappointment at an impossibility to visit the entire section of the magnificent Great Wall.

そこそこで、幅は約40CMしかなく、両側とも切り立った崖になっている。「天橋を過ぎること、青天に上るより難し」が言っている通り、明代長城の中においても最も危険な区間であり、最もひやひやさせる区間である。

司馬台長城は望楼も城壁も奇特で変化に富んでいる。望楼が密集したことは司馬台長城の最大な特徴である。両望楼の間隔は最も近くでわずか43.8M、最も遠いところも600Mしかない。明代には、長城築造に関しては、500Mおきに望楼を造るという規定があるが、これは1つの例外である。望楼の様式は、1穴から5穴までのもの、平屋式のもの、2-3階建てのもの、各階相通じるものと様々なものがある。大小もまちまちで、守備軍の等級、人数と地形に応じて造られている。木造のもののほか、レンガや石を使ったものもある。内部は1部屋、2部屋、多部屋に区切ったものがあり、部屋の配置は「田」字形と「井」字形のものが多い。天井は平面形、アーチ形、八角形と様々なものがある。門や窓の上には美しい文様が彫刻されている。これらのものは、万里の長城の中にはまれにしか見ないもので、観光客をひきつける珠玉の1つとなっている。

果てなく続いて走っていく険しい山々の一側に鴛鴦湖と呼ばれる閑静なダムがある。透き通った水は満々としており、その上は船が行き来している。鴛鴦湖は冷泉と温泉とが会合して出来た人工湖で、氷結することはしない。暑い夏にここに来て船を浮かべて遊べば、暑気がすぐに払い去られてさわやかな気分になる。

司馬台長城は景色が美しいだけでなく、長城の歴史文化を研究するすばらしい宝庫でもある。ここ数年、ここでは数多くの文物が発見されている。たとえば発見した「題名碑」の上には、長城築造の経緯とこれに関連する官員の名前が記されている。ほかに幾つかの区間と望楼では、たとえば「萬暦五年山東左営造」、「萬暦五年寧夏営造」など、長城築造に参加した軍隊の番号や年代を刻んだレンガと石も発見している。これらのレンガや石はレンガづくりの年代、長城築造の監督軍営のほか、長城築造当時の分業をもはっきり教えてくれている。同時に発見した文物にはまた守備部隊が使った鉄砲、石砲、鉄銃、手雷、三眼銃、鉄彈丸、火薬勺などの兵器および鋤、スコップ、包丁、鉄灯碗など守備部隊が使った生産、生活道具がある。これらのものは明代長城と明代の歴史を研究する上で得がたい実物資料である。

著名な長城研究専門家の羅哲文氏は、「中国の長城は世界のトップであり、司馬台長城は中国長城のトップである」と言って司馬台長城を絶賛している。万里の長城は中国人民、ひいては全人類の文化遺産である。司馬台長城はこの貴重な遺産の中の輝かしい真珠である。

司馬台長城が非常に険阻なところにできているもので、観光管理部門は観光客の安全を考えて、12号以上の望楼に登ることを禁止している。本画冊はちょうど、12号以上の望楼に登って美しい景色を実感できない観光客の遺憾の意を補っている。

司馬台長城

司馬台長城は北京市東北120KMの大切な関所・古北口あたりに所在し、明の洪武初年（1368年）に構築されたもので、中国でも最もよく保存された明代長城の区間である。全長は5.4KMで、35の望楼がある。城壁は奇特な発想で設計して構築され、さまざまな形態があり、万里の長城のあらゆる特色を集めているところから、「長城博物館」の称がある。

城壁は険阻な山々に伝わって走っており、「天梯」と「天橋」両区間はそのうちの最も険阻な部分である。「天梯」は切り立った崖に沿って造られた片側城壁のことで、上に立って見下ろすのには、汗を握らせるものがある。「天梯」の突き当たるところは「天橋」である。「天橋」も片側城壁構造のもので、長さは100M

司马台望京楼
The Beijing-Watching Tower on the Simatai Great Wall.
司馬台の望京楼
사마대 망경루
Der Wangjing-Wachtturm der Großen Mauer bei Simatai
La tour de guet Ayant vue sur Beijing.
Simatai: la Torre d'osservazione su Beijing
Torre del Mirador de Beijing

司马台仙女楼
The Fairy Tower on the Simatai Great Wall.
司馬台の仙女楼
사마대 선녀루
Der Xiannü-Wachtturm der Großen Mauer bei Simatai
La tour de guet de la Fée.
Simatai: la Torre della Fata
Torre de Hada

司马台长城

　　司马台长城位于北京东北部120千米的险关重镇古北口境内，始建于明洪武初年（1368年），是至今保留最完整的一段明长城。司马台长城全长5.4千米，有敌楼35座。整段长城构思精巧、设计奇特、形态各异，它集万里长城众多特色于一地，形成了一段"奇妙的长城"，且有"长城博物馆"之称。

　　司马台长城沿刀削斧劈似的山脊修筑，蜿蜒曲折，惊险无比，尤其是天梯和天桥两段。天梯是单面墙长城，坡陡墙窄，最窄处不足半米，呈直梯状沿山体上升，两侧是陡峭悬崖，俯首下望，令人瞠目结舌。天梯顶端便是天桥，长不过百米，只有一块砖那么宽，约40厘米左右，两侧的悬崖绝壁更是令人不寒而栗，到这里的人们都说："过天桥难，难于上青天"，这里是明长城中最险要的地段之一，也是最惊险刺激的地方。

　　司马台长城的敌楼和城墙建筑形式奇特多样，最大的一个特点是敌楼密集，两楼相距最近仅43.8米，最远600米，而其他地方的长城一般都在100米－200米之间。若按明代修筑长城的规定，每500米修敌楼一座，此段长城应该说是一个例外。从外观来看，敌楼有单眼楼、双眼楼、三眼楼、四眼楼和五眼楼，有单层楼，上下相通的双层楼和三层楼。它们均为空心敌楼，大小不一、形态各异，是按驻军的官衔等级、驻防人数以及地势险要程度分别建造的。从内部结构来看，有砖结构、砖木结构、砖石结构；又有单室、双室、多室之分；房间布局有"田"字、"井"字；楼顶形制多样，有平顶、穹窿顶、八角藻井顶、覆斗顶；就连门窗也新颖别致，有边门、中间门、有砖券和石券，还有技艺精湛的雕花花岗岩石门。这些在万里长城中较为罕见，也是吸引游人驻足的亮点。

　　司马台长城虽以山势险峻雄奇为主景，但长城角下的鸳鸯湖却赋予了这段长城以灵性，清澈的湖水造就了一派碧波荡漾、湖光帆影的宁静景观。鸳鸯湖是由冷泉和温泉汇聚而成的，湖水冷暖各半，从不结冰。在炎热的夏季，到这里荡舟湖上，让人暑气顿消，神清气爽。

　　司马台长城不仅有绮丽的风光，更是一座研究长城历史文化遗产的宝库。近年来，这段长城上发现了许多文物。如石刻"题名碑"，碑上记载着当年修建长城时的情况，以及与建城有关的官员的名字，同时在几处城墙和敌楼上还发现带有戳印文字的砖石，上面刻有参加修建长城的军队名称和年代，如"万历五年山东左营造"、"万历五年宁夏营造"等字样。这种带有戳印文字的长城砖除了说明造砖的年代，标明监督的军营，还见证了当年建造长城的明确分工。同时发现的还有一批文物，有明代守城将士使用过的铁炮、石炮、铁镞铁铳、手雷、三眼铳、铁弹丸、火药勺等，还有士兵用过的生产生活用具，如锄头、铁铲、菜刀、铁灯碗等，这些文物为研究明代长城及明代历史提供了很有价值的实物资料。

　　著名长城专家罗哲文曾这样说道："中国长城是世界之最，而司马台长城是中国长城之最。"长城是中国人民，也是全人类的文化遗产，司马台长城则无疑是这份宝贵遗产中光彩熠熠的一颗明珠。

　　由于司马台长城建在地势险要的山巅之上，为保证游客安全，管理部门规定从东12号敌楼向东禁止游客通行。游客已难以领略全段长城的奇绝风光，希望本画册精美的图片能为您弥补些许遗憾。

SIMATAI GREAT WALL

The Simatai section of the Great Wall is situated at Gubeikou, an old town of strategic significance, 120 kilometers northeast of urban Beijing. First built in 1368, the first year during the reign of Emperor Hongwu of the Ming Dynasty (1368-1644), it is among the best-preserved sections of the Great Wall of the Ming Dynasty. The Simatai section spans 5.4 kilometers and has a total of 35 watchtowers. A fantastic section characterized by delicate and unique design and diversified structures, it incorporates a variety of styles of other parts of the Great Wall and is thus reputed as the Museum of the Great Wall.

Zigzagging along steep mountain ranges, this section of the Great Wall features an unmatched peril, especially the two parts respectively called the Heavenly Stairway and the Heavenly Bridge. The Heavenly Stairway, in fact, is a narrow section with a single wall, whose narrowest part is less than half of a meter. The section mounts like a stairway along the mountainside. On both sides are steep and hazardous cliffs, and one would hold breath if he looked down. The Heavenly Bridge, 100 meters in length and some 40 centimeters in width, is situated on the top of the Heavenly Stairway. Cliffs on both sides of the Heavenly Bridge appears to be even more breathtaking. "It is hard to climb onto the Heavenly Bridge—even harder than mounting onto the sky," said some visitors. This part is among the most dangerous but extremely exciting sections of the Great Wall built during the Ming Dynasty.

The walls and watchtowers of the Simatai section of the Great Wall exhibit a unique design and varied architectural styles. One characteristic of this section is its densely-dispersed watchtowers, with the nearest distance of two watchtowers being 43.8 meters and the farthest distance 600 meters. Usually, the nearest distance between two watchtowers is 100-200 meters in other parts of the Great Wall. According to routines of the walls built during the Ming Dynasty, the interval between each two watchtower should be 500 meters. However, the Simatai section is an exception. In the terms of appearance, some watchtowers there have only a single window, and others have two, three, four or five windows; some are one-story structures, and there are also interconnected two- or three-story watchtowers. Various in size and appearance, they were constructed in light of the rank and amount of stationed troops, as well as geographical conditions. Some watchtowers are built with bricks, and others are brick-and-wooden structures or brick-and-stone structures. The watchtowers accommodate one or more chambers. Their roofs are different in design, such as plain roofs, hollow roofs, octagonal painted roofs and reserved-container-shaped roofs. Their gates and windows are also delicately designed, among which include side gates, central gates, brick arches, stone arches and even carved granite gates featuring superb craftsmanship. All of these make Simatai unique among other sections of the Great Wall, thus attracting numerous tourists to visit.

The Simatai section is mainly noted for its magnificent but perilous topography, and meanwhile the Mandarin Duck Lake at the foot of the Great Wall gives this section spirit. The reflections of boat sails on crystal-clear water add a serene and tranquil touch. The lake is where a hot spring and a cold spring meet, so half of its water is warm and the other half is cold. The water never gets frozen there. In scorching summer, boating on the lake is an ideal way to escape from summer heat and get refreshed.

Besides picturesque landscapes, this section of the Great Wall is also a treasure of historical and cultural heritages. In recent years, many historical relics have been unearthed there, including the Stele of Autographs. On the stele is inscribed with information about the construction of the Great Wall as well as the names of officials in charge of

司马台长城入口处
The entrance to the Simatai Great Wall.
司馬台長城の入口
사마대장성 입구
Eingang zur Großen Mauer bei Simatai
Entrée de la Grande Muraille de Simatai.
Simatai: l'accesso alla Grande Muraglia
Entrada de la sección Simatai de la Gran Muralla

construction. On several walls and watchtowers are discovered many bricks and stones with official seals and inscriptions to record the names of troops constructing the Great Wall and the construction time, such as "Constructed by Shandong Left Battalion in the Fifth Year of Emperor Wanli's Reign" and "Constructed by Ningxia Battalion in the Fifth Year of Emperor Wanli's Reign." Besides recording the supervising army and construction time, these inscribed bricks have also witnessed explicit division of labor during the construction of the Great Wall. Among discovered relics also include iron cannons, stone cannons, iron arrowheads, iron guns, iron blunderbusses, grenades, tri-tube guns, iron bullets and powder scoops used troops stationed there, as well as such living appliances and tools as hoes, shovels, kitchen knives and iron lamp bowls. These relics are valuable materials to research the Ming-Dynasty Great Wall and the history of the dynasty.

"The Great Wall is unmatched around the world," said Luo Zhewen, a renowned specialist in research of the Great Wall. "And the Simatai section is unmatched among other sections of the Great Wall." The Great Wall is known as a rare cultural heritage of the Chinese nation and even the whole mankind, and the Simatai section is undoubtedly a brilliant pearl of the cultural heritage.

The Simatai section of the Great Wall is constructed on precipitous mountaintops. For the sake of tourists' safety, therefore, the administrative department of the scenic area has designated the part beyond the No.12 watchtower as a "no-entry zone." We hope this illustrated book will relieve your disappointment at an impossibility to visit the entire section of the magnificent Great Wall.

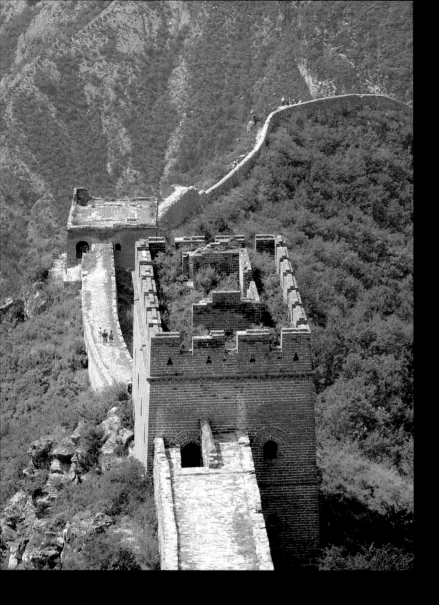

司馬台長城

そこそこで、幅は約40CMしかなく、両側とも切り立った崖になっている。「天橋を過ぎること、青天に上るより難し」が言っている通り、明代長城の中においても最も危険な区間であり、最もひやひやさせる区間である。

司馬台長城は望楼も城壁も奇特で変化に富んでいる。望楼が密集したことは司馬台長城の最大な特徴である。両望楼の間隔は最も近くでわずか43.8M、最も遠いところも600Mしかない。明代には、長城築造に関しては、500Mおきに望楼を造るという規定があるが、これは1つの例外である。望楼の様式は、1穴から5穴までのもの、平屋式のもの、2-3階建てのもの、各階相通じるものと様々なものがある。大小もまちまちで、守備軍の等級、人数と地形に応じて造られている。木造のもののほか、レンガや石を使ったものもある。内部は1部屋、2部屋、多部屋に区切ったものがあり、部屋の配置は「田」字形と「井」字形のものが多い。天井は平面形、アーチ形、八角形と様々なものがある。門や窓の上には美しい文様が彫刻されている。これらのものは、万里の長城の中にはまれにしか見ないもので、観光客をひきつける珠玉の1つとなっている。

果てなく続いて走っていく険しい山々の一側に鴛鴦湖と呼ばれる閑静なダムがある。透き通った水は満々としており、その上は船が行き来している。鴛鴦湖は冷泉と温泉とが会合して出来た人工湖で、氷結することはしない。暑い夏にここに来て船を浮かべて遊べば、暑気がすぐに払い去られてさわやかな気分になる。

司馬台長城は景色が美しいだけでなく、長城の歴史文化を研究するすばらしい宝庫でもある。ここ数年、ここでは数多くの文物が発見されている。たとえば発見した「題名碑」の上には、長城築造の経緯とこれに関連する官員の名前が記されている。ほかに幾つかの区間と望楼では、たとえば「萬暦五年山東左営造」、「萬暦五年寧夏営造」など、長城築造に参加した軍隊の番号や年代を刻んだレンガと石も発見している。これらのレンガや石はレンガづくりの年代、長城築造の監督軍営のほか、長城築造当時の分業をもはっきり教えてくれている。同時に発見した文物にはまた守備部隊が使った鉄砲、石砲、鉄銃、手雷、三眼銃、鉄彈丸、火薬勺などの兵器および鋤、スコップ、包丁、鉄灯碗など守備部隊が使った生産、生活道具がある。これらのものは明代長城と明代の歴史を研究する上で得がたい実物資料である。

著名な長城研究専門家の羅哲文氏は、「中国の長城は世界のトップであり、司馬台長城は中国長城のトップである」と言って司馬台長城を絶賛している。万里の長城は中国人民、ひいては全人類の文化遺産である。司馬台長城はこの貴重な遺産の中の輝かしい真珠である。

司馬台長城が非常に険阻なところにできているもので、観光管理部門は観光客の安全を考えて、12号以上の望楼に登ることを禁止している。本画冊はちょうど、12号以上の望楼に登って美しい景色を実感できない観光客の遺憾の意を補っている。

司馬台長城は北京市東北120KMの大切な関所・古北口あたりに所在し、明の洪武初年（1368年）に構築されたもので、中国でも最もよく保存された明代長城の1区間である。全長は5.4KMで、35の望楼がある。城壁は奇特な発想で設計して構築され、さまざまな形態があり、万里の長城のあらゆる特色を集めているとこ

사마대(司馬臺)장성

베이징에서 북동쪽으로 120km 떨어진 험요한 관문인 고북구(古北口) 경내에 자리한 사마대(司馬臺)장성은 명(明) 홍무 초년(1368년)에 건조되어 오늘까지 완전하게 보전된 명대 장성의 한 구간이다. 사마대장성은 총 길이가 5,400m이며 망루가 35개에 달한다. 구상이 정교하고 설계가 특이하며 형태가 다양한 이 구간 장성은 만리장성의 여러 가지 특색이 한데 집중되어 하나의 '기묘한 장성'을 형성함으로써 이른바 '장성박물관'이라 일컫는다.

사마대장성은 칼로 잘라놓은 듯 한 산등성이를 따라 구불구불 뻗어 있어 매우 험요한데 그중에서도 천제(天梯)와 천교(天橋) 두 구간이 더욱 그러하다. 천제는 단면 벽으로 된 장성으로 성벽이 좁고 가파로운데 제일 좁은 곳은 0.5m 도 안되며 마치 사다리처럼 곧바로 산체를 따라 위로 뻗었고 양쪽은 모두 험한 낭떠러지어서 고개를 숙여 아래를 내려다 보면 눈이 아찔해진다. 천제의 꼭대기에는 천교가 있는데 길이가 근 100m, 너비가 벽돌 한장 정도로 약 40cm 밖에 안되며 양쪽의 깊은 낭떠러지는 더욱 사람들을 몸서리치게 하므로 이곳에 와본 사람들은 '천교를 지나기는 하늘에 오르기보다 더 어렵겠다'고들 한다. 이곳은 명대 장성중에서 제일 험요한 구간의 하나이며 또한 제일 드릴을 자아내는 장소로 꼽힌다.

사마대장성의 망루와 성벽은 건축형식이 특이하고 다양하다. 제일 뚜렷한 특징은 망루가 밀집되어 있는 것인데 두 망루사이의 거리가 제일 가까운 것은 43.8m 밖에 안되며 제일 먼 것도 600m 미만이다. 그러나 다른 지방의 장성은 망루 간격이 일반적으로 100m~200m에 달한다. 만약 명대의 장성 축조규정을 따른다면 망루는 매 500m에 하나씩 건조해야 할 것이지만 이 구간 장성은 예외로 되어있다. 외관으로 보면 이곳 망루에는 단안루 · 쌍안루 · 3안루 · 4안루 · 5안루가 있고 단층루가 있는가 하면 아래 위가 서로 통하는 쌍층루와 3층루도 있다. 이러한 망루는 모두 공심(空心)망루이며 크기가 서로 다르고 형태가 각이한데 이는 주둔군의 관직과 등급, 인원수, 그리고 지세의 험요한 정도에 따라 다르게 건조한 것이다. 내부 구조로 보면 벽돌구조 · 벽돌과 나무 구조 · 벽돌과 돌 구조로 된 것이 있는가 하면 단간 방 · 두간 방 · 여러 간 방으로 되어 있다. 방의 배치로 보면 '川'자형 · '卅'자형으로 되어 있고 망루의 지붕도 다양하여 평평한 지붕 · 아치형 지붕 · 팔각형 지붕 · 복두(覆斗)형 지붕이 있다. 심지어 문창도 유다르고 독특하여 곁문 · 중간문 · 벽돌아치문 · 돌아치문이 있는가 하면 꽃무늬를 조각한 화강암문도 있다. 이러한 것들은 만리장성의 다른 구간에서 보기 드문 깃들이어서 여행객들로 하여금 자주 걸음을 멈추고 살펴보게 한다.

사마대장성은 비록 산세의 험준함과 웅위로움으로 하여 주요 경관을 이루지만 장성밑의 원앙호(鴛鴦湖) 또한 이 구간 장성에 영기(靈氣)를 부여해 주어 맑은 호수물이 끝없이 넘실거리고 그 위로 돛배들이 떠다니는 평온한 광경을 이룬다. 원앙호는 냉천과 온천이 한데 모여 형성된 것으로서 냉수와 온수가 절반씩 차지하므로 호수물이 종내로 얼지 않는다. 무더운 여름철에 이 호수에서 뱃놀이를 하면 삽시에 더위가 가셔지고 기분이 상쾌해진다.

사마대장성은 풍광이 수려할 뿐만 아니라 장성의 역사와 문화유산을 연구하는 보고(寶庫)이기도 하다. 최근년에 이 구간 장성에서는 수많은 문화재가 발견되었다. 이를테면 석각 '제명비(題名碑)'에는 당년에 장성을 축조하던 상황, 장성 축조와 관련된 관리의 이름이 기록되어 있다. 그리고 몇 군데의 성벽과 망루에서 는 인감문자가 찍힌 벽돌이 발견되었는데 그 벽돌에는 장성 축조에 참여한 군대의 명칭과 연대를 기록한 '만력 5년 산동좌영조' · '만력 5년 영하영조'라는 글자가 새겨져 있다. 이렇게 인감문자가 새겨진 장성벽돌은 당시의 연대며 감독에 나섰던 군영을 말해줄 뿐만 아니라 당년 장성 축조 분공이 매우 명확했음을 실증해 준다. 이와 동시에 발견된 문화재로는 또 명대의 장성 경비군이 사용했던 철포 · 석포 · 철촉과 철총 · 수뢰 · 삼안총 · 철탄환 · 화약주걱 등이 있고 병사들이 사용했던 호미 · 삽 · 식칼 · 철제 등잔 등 생산 및 생활 도구가 있다. 이러한 문화재들은 명대 장성 및 명대 역사를 연구하는데 매우 가치있는 실물자료로 된다.

이름난 장성 전문가 뤄저원(羅哲文)은 "중국의 장성은 세계의 제일이며 사마대 장성은 또한 중국 장성의 제일이다."라고 말했다. 장성은 중국인민, 나아가 전인류의 문화유산이며 사마대장성은 당연히 이 귀중한 문화유산중의 눈부신 명주로 된다.

사마대장성은 지세가 험요한 산정에 축조되어 있으므로 여행객들의 안전을 보장하기 위하여 관리부처에서는 동 12루서부터 여행객들의 통행을 금지하도록 규정했다. 여행객들은 이미 전 구간의 기이한 풍광을 다 감지하기 어렵게 되었으므로 본 화첩의 정미한 사진들이 그 아쉬움을 덜어드리게 되기를 희망한다.

Die Große Mauer bei Simatai

Die Große Mauer bei Simatai ist der am vollständigsten erhaltene Abschnitt der weltbekannten Großen Mauer aus der Ming-Zeit. Sie liegt innerhalb des alten Passes Gubeikou im Nordosten der Kreisstadt Miyun, 120 km von dem Stadtgebiet Beijings entfernt, und wird auch Simatai-Mauer genannt. Sie wurde im ersten Jahre (1368) der Hongwu-Regierungsperiode der Ming-Dynastie (1368-1644) gebaut, ist 5,4 km lang und hat insgesamt 35 Wachttürme. Sie zeichnet sich durch die feine Konstruktion, den eigenartigen Entwurf und die verschiedenartigen Formen aus. Sie konzentriert Besonderheiten der anderen Abschnitte der Großen Mauer, bildet einen „wunderbaren" Mauerabschnitt und wird daher als „Museum der Großen Mauer" bezeichnet.

Die Simatai-Mauer schlängelt sich durch Bergrücken und ist besonders schwer passierbar. Erwähnenswert sind die Mauerabschnitte Tianti „Himmelsleiter" und Tianqiao „Himmelsbrücke". Sie sind jeweils nur etwa 40 bis 50 cm breit. An beiden Seiten dieser Mauerabschnitte sieht man tiefe Schluchten. Wer durch diese Mauerabschnitte geht, läuft ihm ein Schauder über den Rücken.

Bei Simatai sieht man im Abstand von 43,8 bis 600 Metern einen Wachttrum, in anderen Abschnitten der Großen Mauer gibt es aber durchschnittlich im Abstand von 100 bis 200 Metern einen Wachtturm. Der historischen Überlieferung zufolge sollte der Abstand zwischen zwei Wachttürmen 500 Meter sein. So kann man sagen, dass die Simatai-Mauer eine Seltenheit ist. Normalerweise hat jeder Wachtturm zwei Geschosse. Das Erdgeschoss diente als Stationierungsort für Soldaten und gleichzeitig als Waffen- und Munitionslager. Das mit einer oder zwei, drei, vier und fünf Schießscharten ausgestatte Obergeschoss stand den Wächtern zur Verfügung. Diese Wachttürme sind verschiedenförmig: Sie sind viereckig, kreisförmig oder plattförmig. Ihre Decken sind ebenfalls verschiedenförmig. Sie sind flach, gewölbt oder segel- oder kassettenförmig. An beiden Seiten jedes Wachtturmes gibt es jeweils eine 2,5 Meter hohe Sperrauer mit Schießscharten. Diese Wachttürme wurden damals aus Ziegel, Holz und Stein gebaut. Heute sieht man drinnen 田 - und 井-förmige Räume. Jeder Wachtturm hat ein bogenförmiges Neben- oder ein Mitteltor aus Ziegel und oder Stein mit geschnitzten Blumenmustern.

Die Landschaft in Simatai ist das ganze Jahr hindurch sehr faszinierend: Im Frühling, wenn Pfirsichbäume und Aprikosenbäume blühen, sieht Simatai wie ein Blumenmeer aus. Im Sommer steht das ganze Gebirgsgebiet in saftigem Grün. Besonders nach dem Regen sieht man hier oft Regenbogen. Im Herbst leuchten die Ahornblätter an Berghängen in den verschiedensten Rottönen. Im Winter sieht Simatai wie eine Schneewelt aus, auf der sich die Große Mauer wie eine riesige Schlange schlängelt. Eine andre Attraktion bei Simatai ist der „Mandarinenente-See" am Bergfuß. Er wird von einer kalten und einer heißen Quelle gespeichert und ist im Winter eisfrei. Eine Schiffsfahrt durch diesen See ist im Sommer besonders empfehlenswert.

Die Simatai-Mauer ist eine Schatzkammer für das Studium der Geschichte der Großen Mauer. In den letzten Jahren haben chinesische Archäologen hier viele kostbare Kulturgegenstände wie Geschütze, Steinwaffen, Pfeilspitzen, Artilleriegeschosse aus Stein oder Eisen sowie Gebrauchsartikel und Produktionswerkzeuge wie Küchenmesser, Steinmörser, Öllampen, Hacken und Schaufeln freigelegt. In der Nähe des „Weißen Wachtturmes" sieht man zahlreiche Mauerziegel mit chinesischen Schriftzeichen, die angeben, wann diese Ziegel hergestellt und gebrannt wurden.

Luo Zhewen, ein bekannter chinesischer Expert für die Große Mauer, hat so gesagt: „Die Große Mauer ist weltbekannt, ihr Abschnitt bei Simatai ist aber am bekanntesten. " Heute ist die Simatai-Mauer ein Schwerpunkt des Denkmalschutzes und wurde schon in die UNESCO-Liste des Weltkulturerbes aufgenommen. Als eine große Attraktion der Stadt Beijing zieht sie immer mehr in- und ausländische Touristen an.

Die Große Mauer bei Simatai liegt auf den schwer zugänglichen Gebirgskämmen. Sicherheitshalber darf man von dem Wachtturm Nr. 12 an nicht auf sie steigen. Daher kann man hier nicht die ganze Mauerstrecke bewundern. Möge dieser Bildband Ihnen bei Ihrer Simatai-Reise ein hilfreicher Begleiter sein.

La Grande Muraille de Simatai

Située aux environs de la ville de Gubeikou, connue pour être une passe difficile à franchir et une position d'importance stratégique, la Grande Muraille de Simatai dont la construction débuta en première année du règne Hongwu de la dynastie des Ming est jusqu'ici le tronçon le mieux préservé de la Grande Muraille des Ming. La Grande Muraille de Simatai possède 35 tours de guet sur sa longueur totale de 5,4 km. D'une conception ingénieuse et originale et ayant la forme très variée, elle incarne de façon concentrée les particularités caractéristiques de la Grande Muraille longue de 10 000 *li* (1 *li* égal à 0,5 km), raison pour laquelle elle est réputée "Grande Muraille merveilleuse" et "Musée de Grande Muraille".

Construite sur les crêtes des montagnes, la Grande Muraille de Simatai est fort sinueuse et d'un accès à couper le souffle, notamment le tronçon de l'Escalier menant au ciel et celui de la Passerelle. L'Escalier menant au ciel est constitué par un mur simple très mince dont l'épaisseur est moins de 0,5 m à certains endroits. Elle s'élève à pic sur les falaises abruptes. Quand on regarde d'en haut vers le bas, on est frappé de stupéfaction. Au-delà de l'Escalier menant au ciel est la Passerelle qui ne s'étire que sur une centaine de mètres. Aussi large qu'une brique, le haut du mur n'est que d'une quarantaine de centimètres de largeur. Les falaises en surplomb des deux côtés font frémir de crainte. Les gens qui y montent ne peuvent s'empêcher de pousser des cris d'épouvante. "Passer sur la Passerelle est plus difficile que de monter au ciel !" disent de nombreuses personnes. C'est l'un des tronçons les plus périlleux et les plus excitants de la Grande Muraille des Ming !

La forme architecturale des remparts et des tours de guet de la Grande Muraille de Simatai est aussi variée qu'originale. Sa particularité la plus importante réside dans la densité de forteresses. Les deux tours de guet les plus proches l'une de l'autre ne sont distantes que de 43,8 m, tandis que l'intervalle entre les deux voisines les plus éloignées est de 600 m. Mais dans les autres endroits, la distance entre les deux tours voisines varie entre 100 et 200 m. Etant donné que sous les Ming, on a prévu la construction d'une tour de guet tous les 500 m sur la Grande Muraille, le tronçon de Simatai doit être une exception. A en juger par leurs apparences, les tours de guet sont munies chacune d'une à cinq ouvertures, sans ou avec un ou deux étages. Ces tours de guet creuses, dont les tailles sont différentes et la forme variée, furent bâties selon le grade de l'officier de la garnison, le nombre des soldats et la situation géographique des différents lieux. A en juger par leurs structures internes, ces tours sont en briques, en briques et bois ou en briques et pierre. Chaque tour comprend une, deux ou plusieurs pièces. Dans ce dernier cas, celles-ci sont disposées en caractère " 田 " ou " 井 ". Les formes des couvertures des tours de guet sont également variées. On y voit des toits plats ou en dôme, des plafonds à caissons octogonaux et des toitures évoquant un boisseau renversé. Même les portes et les fenêtres ont été ingénieusement réalisées. On trouve des portes latérales, des portes centrales, voûtées en briques ou en pierre, voire des portes en granit finement sculpté. Tout cela constitue le centre d'intérêts des visiteurs.

Bien que la Grande Muraille de Simatai aient les falaises abruptes et les précipices escarpés pour les attractions essentielles, le lac des Canards mandarins s'étendant à son pied ajoute encore à son charme. D'innombrables barques à voile cahotent sur l'eau émeraude qui ondule sur le lac. Ce dernier, alimenté par une source froide et une source chaude, ne gèle jamais. Si l'on y fait une promenade en été, on a une sensation de fraîcheur très agréable.

La Grande Muraille de Simatai non seulement offre un paysage magnifique, mais est aussi un grand trésor pour étudier le brillant héritage culturel et historique lié à la Grande Muraille. Au cours de ces dernières années, de nombreux objets anciens et vestiges historiques ont été découverts sur la Grande Muraille de Simatai, comme par exemple la stèle monumentale aux inscriptions racontant les détails de la construction de la Grande Muraille et mentionnant les noms des officiers et des fonctionnaires concernés. Dans les murs et les tours de guet à différents endroits ont aussi été découvertes des briques et des pierres sur lesquelles sont gravées les désignations des unités militaires entreprenant des travaux et les dates telles que "Fabriquée en l'an 5 du règne Wangli (des Ming) par le bataillon de la Gauche du Shandong", "Fabriquée en l'an 5 du règne Wangli par le bataillon du Ningxia", etc. Non seulement ces inscriptions indiquent les dates de la fabrication des briques et les noms des unités militaires chargées de la supervision, mais donnent aussi des renseignements sur la répartition des travaux à la tâche. Y ont également été retrouvés des mortiers de fer et de pierre, des tromblons de fer, des fers de flèche, des grenades, des tromblons à trois tubes, des projectiles de fer, des louches à poudre ainsi que des ustensiles d'usage courant et des moyens de production tels que les houes, les pelles, les couteaux de cuisine, des fers de lampe à huile et bien d'autres encore, utilisés par les soldats des Ming. Tous ces objets sont autant de matériaux en nature d'une grande valeur pour étudier la Grande Muraille et l'histoire des Ming.

Luo Zhewen, fameux expert spécialisé dans l'étude de la Grande Muraille, a dit : "La Grande Muraille de Chine est l'ouvrage le plus gigantesque du monde et le tronçon de Simatai, le plus spectaculaire de la Grande Muraille de Chine." La Grande Muraille fait partie du patrimoine culturel du peuple chinois, mais aussi de celui de toute l'humanité. La Grande Muraille de Simatai est sans doute un élément rayonnant d'éclat de cet héritage précieux.

Du fait que la Grande Muraille de Simatai a été construite sur les crêtes des montagnes qui sont difficiles d'accès, pour rassurer la sécurité des visiteurs, le département d'administration a décidé d'interdire à toute personne d'accéder à la section au-delà de la tour de guet N° 12. Désormais, il est difficile aux visiteurs de goûter la beauté exceptionnelle de l'ensemble de la Grande Muraille de Simatai. Nous espérons que les belles photos du présent album contribueront à réparer quelque peu vos regrets dûs à cette interdiction.

La Grande Muraglia di Simatai

A 120 chilometri a nord-est di Pechino, in una posizione strategica molto importante sul territorio della contea di Gubeikou, si estende il tratto della Muraglia di Simatai, la cui edificazione ebbe inizio nel primo anno del regno dell'imperatore Hongwu (1368) della dinastia Ming. Si tratta di un tratto ben conservato di Muraglia risalente alla dinastia Ming, sulla cui complessiva lunghezza di 5,4 chilometri, si ergono 35 torri di guardia.

La raffinatezza della fortificazione e la singolarità del progetto, dalle svariate soluzioni architettoniche, costituiscono le peculiarità della Muraglia di Simatai, in cui sono sintetizzate le caratteristiche di diversi tratti di Muraglia lungo i diecimila *li* di lunghezza di questa imponente costruzione, tutto ciò rende quello di Simatai uno dei tratti più particolari della Muraglia cinese, noto col nome di "Museo della Grande Muraglia".

Edificata lungo la cresta del monte, la serpeggiante Muraglia di Simatai ha un aspetto maestoso, soprattutto nei due tratti chiamati *Tianti* e *Tianqiao*. Il primo è costituito da un muro molto stretto e ripido, la cui parte più stretta non arriva a 50 cm di larghezza. Esso scala il monte protendendosi verso l'alto come una scala di cui i lati si affacciano su scoscesi precipizi. Guardando dal basso verso l'alto si ha una sensazione di smarrimento ed insieme di paura. Il tratto *Tianqiao* che è lungo 100 metri e largo 40 cm, è situato più in alto rispetto al tratto *Tianti*. I precipizi su cui si affaccia il tratto *Tianqiao* sono ancora più ripidi di quelli del tratto *Tianti*. C'è chi dice che la Muraglia a *Tianqiao* è così ripida che la scalata sembra quasi un'ascesa al cielo. Questo è il tratto più maestoso ed impressionante della Muraglia di epoca Ming.

Sulla Grande Muraglia di Simatai si trovano numerose torri di guardia costruite non lontane l'una dall'altra, in diversi stili architettonici. La distanza più breve fra di esse è di 43,8 metri, mentre quella maggiore è di 600 metri. Di solito la distanza fra due torri di guardia lungo la Muraglia varia fra i 100 ed i 200 metri. Secondo il progetto di epoca Ming, relativo alla costruzione della Grande Muraglia, la distanza fra due torri di guardia

doveva essere di 500 metri, per cui questo tratto costituisce un'eccezione. Le torri di guardia erano costituite da uno, due o tre piani e potevano avere da una a cinque finestre. All'interno vi sono vani vuoti, le cui dimensioni e forme differiscono, a seconda del grado dell'ufficiale dell'esercito che vi risiedeva, del numero dei soldati che vi facevano la guardia e della posizione geografica in cui erano state edificate. La loro struttura fu realizzata con materiale edile diverso: solo in mattoni, mattoni e legno oppure mattoni e pietra. Alcune sono composte da una sola stanza, altre da due o più stanze la cui distribuzione all'interno si ispira alla forma dei caratteri cinesi " 田 " *tian* di "campo" e *jing* " 井 " di "pozzo". Anche la forma del tetto varia, vi sono coperture piane, a volta, a cassettoni ottagonali, ecc. Le porte e le finestre hanno diverse caratteristiche, a volte sono laterali, a volte sono centrali, ad arco in mattoni o in pietra, oppure realizzate in granito con figure scolpite. Tutto ciò rende questo tratto di Muraglia molto interessante per i visitatori ed unico lungo i diecimila *li* di questa costruzione.

Le principali attrattive della Grande Muraglia di Simatai sono la sua maestosità e la sua posizione, inerpicata lungo la cresta della montagna lungo pendii scoscesi. Il lago dell'Anatra Selvatica ai piedi della Grande Muraglia di Simatai è un altro elemento molto affascinante. Le acque del lago provengono sia da sorgenti d'acqua fredda che da sorgenti d'acqua termale, le acque delle due sorgenti mescolandosi fanno si che questo lago non ghiacci mai. Questo è il luogo ideale dove trovare sollievo durante le afose giornate estive di Beijing. Oltre a costituire un meraviglioso paesaggio, la Grande Muraglia di Simatai è un "museo" di tesori per lo studio del patrimonio culturale e storico. Negli ultimi anni, lungo la Muraglia di Simatai sono stati portati alla luce numerosi reperti archeologici come, per esempio, una stele con iscrizioni d'epoca su cui sono riportati dati sulla costruzione della Muraglia ed i nomi degli ufficiali che parteciparono alla sua realizzazione, inoltre sono stati ritrovati dei mattoni con iscrizioni e sigilli sui quali sono incisi il nome dell'esercito che fabbricò i mattoni e quello dell'esercito che costruì le mura. Ecco alcuni esempi delle iscrizioni ritrovate: "Edificato dal battaglione Zuo dello Shandong nel quinto anno del regno dell'imperatore Wanli", "Edificato dal battaglione del Ningxia nel quinto anno del regno dell'imperatore Wanli", ecc. Questi mattoni con iscrizioni riportano non solo la data di realizzazione dei mattoni stessi ed i nomi dei battaglioni che edificarono la Muraglia, ma anche l'organizzazione del lavoro durante la costruzione. Sono state inoltre ritrovate armi di diverso tipo: cannoni di ferro e di pietra, frecce di ferro, spingarde di ferro, rudimentali bombe a mano, spingarde a tre fori, palle di cannone in ferro, cucchiai per prendere la polvere da sparo ed altro materiale bellico, insieme a numerosi altri oggetti di uso quotidiano appartenuti ai soldati ed ai generali, fra cui: zappe, pale di ferro, coltelli da cucina, lampade di ferro, scodelle ed altro ancora. Tutti questi ritrovamenti sono molto importanti non solo per lo studio e la documentazione storica della Grande Muraglia di epoca Ming, ma anche per lo studio della dinastia Ming stessa.

Luo Zhewen, un noto esperto e studioso della Grande Muraglia di epoca Ming, ha detto: "La Grande Muraglia è il monumento più bello del mondo, il tratto di Simatai è il più bello dell'intera Muraglia cinese". La Grande Muraglia cinese è infatti un importante patrimonio culturale non soltanto per il popolo cinese, ma per tutta l'umanità. La Muraglia di Simatai è senza alcun dubbio una splendida perla fra i patrimoni culturali mondiali.

A causa della sua posizione pericolosa in cima alla collina e al fine di garantire la sicurezza dei turisti, il Dipartimento amministrativo del turismo ha deciso di non permettere l'accesso oltre la Torre di Gurdia N.12 del tratto della Grande muraglia di Simatai. Per questo motivo i turisti non potranno ammirare il meraviglioso paesaggio di questo tratto. Speriamo, attraverso le belle immagini del nostro album, di sopperire in qualche modo al dispiacere determinato da questo regolamento.

La Gran Muralla en Simatai

La sección Simatai de la Gran Muralla pasa por Gubeikou, poblado y paso de suma importancia estratégica al noreste de Beijing, a 120 km del centro urbano de la capital. Dicha sección data de 1368, primer año del reinado del emperador Hongwu. Es también la más original y mejor preservada hasta hoy del período de la dinastía Ming en toda la Gran Muralla. A lo largo de sus 5,4 km, se distribuyen 35 atalayas y se pueden observar casi todas las peculiaridades arquitectónicas del mencionado monumento, gracias a lo cual ha merecido los títulos de "segmento extraordinario" y "Museo de la Gran Muralla".

Entre los tramos que serpentean por las escarpadas crestas montañosas se encuentran los denominados "escalera al cielo" y "puente al cielo," los cuales se refieren a dos de los trechos de más difícil acceso. En el primer caso, la muralla sólo cuenta con un parapeto en uno de sus lados, mientras que su sección más angosta mide menos de 50 cm. Desde arriba se ve algo que semeja una escalera vertical, en la cual se apoya la pendiente. A la "escalera" sigue el "puente al cielo". Se trata de un camino de unos 100 m. de largo, pero con sólo una losa de ancho – de unos 40 cm. Debajo se extienden precipicios y valles profundos. No en balde se ha extendido el dicho local de que "es más fácil ir al cielo que pasar el puente al cielo". A ellos también obedece la fama de Simatai como tramo más peligroso y estratégico de la Gran Muralla, que al mismo tiempo resulta el más fascinante para los exploradores.

Las atalayas, así como otras estructuras arquitectónicas que se distribuyen en este segmento ostentan formas muy variadas y singulares y se caracterizan por su alta densidad constructiva. Aquí las atalayas más cercanas sólo distan 43,8 m y las más lejanas, 600 m, mientras en el resto de la Gran Muralla la distancia promedio oscila entre 100 y 200 m. Estas medidas, sin embargo, no se corresponden con las pautas de la dinastía Ming, según las cuales la mayor separación entre dos atalayas no puede sobrepasar los 500 m. Cabe aclarar que este tramo es una excepción. Hay atalayas de solo uno, dos, tres, cuatro y hasta cinco agujeros, y de uno, dos y tres pisos. Todas son huecas y sus tamaños y formas varían en dependencia del rango del jefe militar que las ocupaba, así como el número de guardias y el nivel de importancia estratégica del lugar. Según su estructura interior, las atalayas se dividen en las hechas de ladrillos, en ladrillo y madera y en ladrillo y piedra. Las salas internas pueden ser una, dos o varias, y cuentan con una distribución diferente. Los techos se construyeron en forma tradicional aunque con gran variedad de estilos. Incluso las ventanas y puertas lucen diseños singulares, ya sean laterales o centrales, en ladrillo, piedra o granito, en los cuales no faltan las minuciosas decoraciones o hermosos bajorrelieves. El carácter único de edificaciones como estas dotan a la Gran Muralla de un atractivo especial que se erige en punto de atracción para los turistas.

En Simatai, además de disfrutar del majestuoso paisaje montañoso, los visitantes también pueden deleitarse con la hermosura del lago al pie de la Gran Muralla. Bautizado como Yuanyang – pato mandarín, que en China es símbolo de pareja afectuosa –, el lago posee un agua transparente y serena. La misma proviene de dos fuentes, una termal y otra fría, lo que incide que el lago sea mitad tibio y mitad frío. En invierno el lago nunca se congela, mientras que en verano es ideal para acampar.

Simatai no sólo ofrece su belleza natural, es a la vez un depósito de tesoros para la investigación histórica y cultural de la Gran Muralla. En años recientes se han descubierto muchas reliquias antiguas en esta sección. Por ejemplo, hay una estela de piedra sobre la cual se inscribieron los nombres de los funcionarios a cargo de la construcción de las murallas y se describieron las labores para su construcción. Además, en los parapetos y varias atalayas se localizaron los ladrillos con inscripciones del año y denominación de la unidad militar encargada de levantar los muros. Se han hallado también las armas usadas por los soldados de la dinastía Ming, incluidos cañones de hierro y de piedra, fusiles, granadas, balas, etc, y los utensilios de vida y producción agrícola, como azadas, paletas y cuchillos. Todos estos descubrimientos han aportado valiosas pruebas para los estudios de la dinastía Ming y de la Gran Muralla.

Luo Zhewen, famoso experto en el tema de la Gran Muralla, considera que la misma no tiene parangón en el mundo, mientras que Simatai no tiene igual dentro de la Gran Muralla, tanto en belleza como en relevancia histórica.

En su sección de Simatai, la Gran Muralla pasa principalmente por las montañas de acceso difícil y peligroso. Con el fin de garantizar la seguridad de los turistas, las administraciones locales han prohibido el paso de los visitantes desde la Atalaya Doce. Por eso ustedes ya no pueden disfrutar personalmente del impresionante paisaje de toda la sección y a lo mejor podrán compensar de alguna manera esta pérdida con este folleto ilustrado.

鸳鸯泉

Mandarin Duck Springs

在司马台西段长城根下常年流淌着水温38℃左右的温泉，令人称奇的是在相距几十米的东山根下，却是冰冷刺骨的冷泉。这鬼斧神工、奇景天成的泉水，当地叫它"鸳鸯泉"。据地质专家考证，这股冷泉是通往雾灵山的一条地下水脉，时隔50余年才能渗透到这里。所以，冷泉流量的大小，取决于50年前雾灵山地区的旱涝。1977年，密云县政府在司马台长城脚下修建了一座司马台水库，水库面积2.3公顷，库容57.2万立方米。库水就是由温泉与冷泉汇集而成。水库建成后，这里又多了一道特殊的风景线。尤其是春、夏、秋三季，在阳光照射下，湖水波光粼粼，清澈见底，山峦、树木、长城倒映在水中，再加上时而飞来的野鸭子、水鸟，形成了长城与山水风光交相辉映的画卷。(P18—P21)

At the foot of the western Simatai section of the Great Wall is running a hot spring, with a perennial temperature around 38ºC. It is astonishing that there is another spring with chilly water at the foot of the Eastern Hill that is only dozens of meters away. A wonder of nature, the two springs are popularly called the Mandarin Duck Springs. According to research of geologists, the cold spring takes its source at water penetrating from an underground river in the Wuling Mountain, and it takes 50 years to come here. Therefore, its amount of water depends on the rainfalls of the Wuling Mountain area 50 years ago. In 1977, the government of Miyun County constructed a reservoir at the foot of the Simatai section, which covers 2.3 hectares and has a capacity of 572,000 cubic meters. The water in the reservoir is provided by said two springs. After its completion, the reser-

长城脚下的司马台水库
The Simatai Reservoir at the foot of the Great Wall.
長城ふもとの司馬台ダム
장성기슭에 자리한 사마대저수지
Der Simatai-Staubecken am Fuß der Großen Mauer
Réservoir d'eau de Simatai au pied de la Grande Muraille.
Il bacino artificiale di Simatai ai piedi della Grande Muraglia
Represa de Simatai

voir has become a new scenic spot. In spring, summer and autumn, the clear water shines under the sunlight, and surrounding hills, trees and the Great Wall are reflected on the water. In addition to wild ducks and other waterfowls flying around, the reservoir presents a natural picture in which the Great Wall and the surrounding landscapes set off each other.(P18-P21)

積2.3ha、貯水量57.2万㎥の司馬台ダムを造って、長城周辺にもう1ヵ所の景勝地を添えている。毎年の春、夏と秋に、湖面上のさざなみが日に照らされてピカピカしていて、周辺の山々や木々、長城の城壁、および時には飛んできた水鳥や鴨などとともに、美しい山水の絵巻を作り上げている。(P18-P21)

鴛鴦泉

司馬台長城の西段に一年中38℃に保っている温泉が湧いており、これと反して数10M離れた東山には肌を刺すような冷泉が流れている。土地の人々はこの2つの大自然の傑作を「鴛鴦泉」と呼んでいる。地質専門家の調査によれば、冷泉は霧霊山から源を持っているもので、50年経ってはじめてやっとここに流れてきたと言われている。だからその流量は完全に上流地の増水や旱魃に左右されている。1977年、密雲県政府はこの温泉と冷泉の水を集めて、長城のふもとに水面

원앙천

사마대의 서쪽 구간 장성밑에는 일년 내내 38℃의 온수가 흐르는 온천이 있고 온천에서 몇십 미터 떨어진 동산기슭에는 기이하게도 얼음같이 차가운 냉천이 있다. 신비로운 이 두 샘물을 당지에서는 '원앙천(鴛鴦泉)'이라고 부른다. 지질학자의 고증에 따르면 이 냉천은 무령산(霧靈山)으로 통하는 한 갈래의 지하수맥으로서 50여년이 걸려 이곳에 침투된 것이라고 한다. 때문에 냉천의 유량은 50년 전 무령산지구의 가뭄과 장마에 달리게 된다. 1977년 미원(密雲)현 정부는 사

마대장성 기슭에다 사마대저수지를 건설했는데 저수지 면적은 2.3 헥타르, 저수량은 57 만 2,000 ㎥에 달한다. 저수지 물은 온천과 냉천이 한데 모여 이루어졌다. 저수지가 건설됨에 따라 이곳에는 또 하나의 독특한 풍경지가 이루어졌다. 특히 봄· 여름· 가을 세 계절이면 눈부신 햇빛아래 맑은 호수물이 금빛으로 넘실거리고 맑은 물속에 산발· 수목· 장성의 그림자가 거꾸로 비치는 데다 이따금 물오리떼며 물새들이 날아와 장성과 호수풍광이 아름답게 어우러진 산수화를 형성한다. (P18-P21)

précipitations annuelles 50 ans auparavant dans les monts Wuling. En 1977, le gouvernement du district de Miyun a fait construire au pied de la Grande Muraille de Simatai un réservoir s'étendant sur 2,3 ha et d'une capacité de 572 000 m³ d'eau. Alimenté par les sources chaude et froide, ce réservoir constitue un nouveau site pittoresque. Notamment au printemps, en été et en automne, la brise fait à la surface du réservoir des rides d'un bleu limpide qui scintillent au soleil. Les montagnes, les arbres et la Grande Muraille, qui se réfléchissent dans l'eau, ainsi que des canards sauvages et d'autres oiseaux aquatiques qui y viennent de temps à l'autre composent un tableau de paysage splendide. (P18-P21)

Yuanyangquan

Bei Yuanyangquan handelt es sich um eine heiße und eine kalte Quelle. Die heiße Quelle liegt am Fuß des westlichen Mauerabschnitts. Ihre Temperatur liegt das ganze Jahr hindurch bei etwa 38°C. Die kalte Quelle liegt am Fuß des Dongshan-Berges, Duzende Meter von der heißen Quelle entfernt. Geografische Untersuchungen beweisen, dass diese kalte Quelle im Wuling-Gebirge entspringt. Es braucht mindestens 50 Jahre, bis das Quellwasser von dort hierher fließt. Ihre Durchflussmenge hängt daher davon ab, wie groß die Niederschlagsmenge im Wuling-Gebirge vor 50 Jahren war. Im Jahre 1977 wurde hier ein Staubecken errichtet. Er nimmt eine Fläche von 2,3 ha ein und hat eine Fassungskapazität von 572 000 Kubikmetern. Neben Regenwasser bilden die beiden Quellen seine Wasserquelle. Heute ist dieser künstliche See nicht nur eine touristische Attraktion, sondern auch ein Paradies für wilde Enten und andere Wasservögel. (P18-P21)

Les sources des Canards mandarins

Au pied de la partie ouest de la Grande Muraille de Simatai coule en permanence l'eau d'une température d'environ 38 °C, jaillie d'une source chaude, tandis qu'au pied d'une montagne à des dizaines de mètres à l'est de la première se trouve une autre source dont l'eau est d'un froid pénétrant. Les habitants locaux les appellent "sources des Canards mandarins" Les géologues révèlent que cette source froide est alimentée par une veine d'eau partant des monts Wuling, dont l'eau doit mettre 50 ans pour s'infiltrer dans cette source le long de ladite veine, ce qui signifie que le débit de la source froide dépend des

La fonte dell'Anatra Selvatica

Ad occidente ai piedi della Grande Muraglia di Simatai, sgorga una fonte d'acque termali la cui temperatura arriva a 38°C. Ai piedi della parte orientale della Muraglia, ad alcune decine di metri di distanza dalla prima, sgorga una fonte d'acqua fredda. La gente del posto chiama questo il lago dell'Anatra selvatica (Yuanyang).

Secondo quanto affermano i geologi, la fonte d'acqua fredda scorre lungo il fiume sotterraneo situato sotto il monte Wuling, per aprirsi il percorso fino a Simatai l'acqua ha impiegato 50 anni e la portata del corso è variata nel tempo a seconda della siccità e delle piogge nella zona montana di Wuling. Nel 1977, il governo distrettuale di Miyun costruì un bacino artificiale a Simatai che copre una superficie di 2,3 ettari ed ha una capacità di 572.000 metri cubi d'acqua. Le acque del bacino hanno origine dalle due fonti d'acqua calda e fredda. Dopo la sua costruzione, il serbatoio è diventato un'attrazione turistica rinomata. In primavera, estate ed autunno, sotto la luce del sole, le acque del bacino sono così limpide che si può vedere chiaramente il fondo dell'invaso, i monti e gli alberi si riflettono sulla superficie dell'acqua, le anatre selvatiche e gli uccelli acquatici, costituiscono, insieme alla Muraglia, un paesaggio incantevole simile ad un rotolo di pittura tradizionale cinese.(P18-P21)

Manantiales de Yuanyang

Al oeste de Simatai, hay un manantial termal cuyas aguas mantienen una temperatura de alrededor de 38°. Lo curioso es que, a sólo decenas de metros de distancia, hay otra fuente de agua helada al pie de la montaña. Ambos surtidores han sido denominados "Manantiales de Yuanyang".Según los geólogos, el origen de la fuente fría es el agua subterránea debajo de una montaña cercana, la cual demora 50 años en infiltrar a la fuente, de ahí que el volumen del agua varíe según la cantidad de precipitación caída 50 años atrás en la montaña. En 1977, el gobierno local del distrito Miyun construyó aquí una represa de 2,3 ha de superficie y 57,2m³ de capacidad, con el agua proveniente de la fuente termal y la helada. La represa ha pasado a ser nuevo punto de atracción de la zona, sobre todo en primavera, verano y otoño, cuando el sol ilumina el agua transparente del lago, reflejando la montaña sobre su superficie, donde se perciben asimismo el bosque y la Gran Muralla. A vista tan bucólica se suman las bandadas de aves salvajes que pululan en el sitio.(P18-P21)

在水库岸边远望司马台东段长城
The eastern section of the Simatai Great Wall viewed from the bank of the Simatai Reservoir.
ダムの一角から見た司馬台長城東段
저수지기슭에서 멀리 바라본 사마대 동쪽 구간 장성
Der östliche Mauerabschnitt, von dem Ufer des Simatai-Staubeckens aus gesehen
Partie est de la Grande Muraille de Simatai, un cliché réalisé depuis le bord du réservoir.
Il lato orientale della Grande Muraglia di Simatai, veduta dal bacino artificiale
La Gran Muralla de la línea oriental

东二楼

明敌楼损毁严重，残存的部分墙体也摇摇欲坠。这座敌楼是木梁柱结构，木料虽已腐烂无存，但古镜式柱础石和墙体上残存的柱洞依然清晰可见。相传，这是戚继光创建空心敌台的最初式样。空心敌台坚固、实用，它可以宿兵贮器，传递信息，战斗中便于左右呼应，极大地完善了长城的防御功能。

除东二楼以外，司马台长城的木梁柱结构敌楼还有七座，主要分布在长城西段。据专家推测，这种结构的敌楼建于明朝隆庆年间（1567年——1572年）。据史料记载，隆庆年间所建木梁柱结构的空心敌台，每座台用工总计约4.5万工作日。总督谭伦在给皇帝的奏疏中这样说道：“（敌台）今其规制迥曰昔时，所资人力，五百名三月之久仅完台一座。”朝廷“（每台）所给官银五十两，不足以供雇募匠役之费”。说明当年修建长城的民工大部分是招募而来的，其中有木匠、石匠、砖、灰窑匠、铁匠、瓦匠，甚至有油匠、画匠，分工非常细致，但主要劳动力仍然是军队士兵。(P22-P26)

東二楼

明代望楼のほとんどは酷く壊され、残った城壁部分も今にも倒そうな状態になっている。東二楼は木造のものであって、木製の桁や梁は腐っていて、もはや存在していないが、柱の礎石と壁に残った柱穴はやはりはっきり見出すことが出来る。言い伝えでは、東二楼は戚継光が開発した中空式望楼の最初の様式である。堅固実用で、守備部隊の宿泊地としても兵器貯蔵室としてもよく、情報伝達や作戦時の相互連絡にも便利な中空式望楼は、長城の防御機能を大いに引き上げた。

東二楼のほかに、司馬台長城にはまた7ヵ所の木造望楼があり、主に長城の西段に分布している。専門家たちは、これらの木造望楼が明の隆慶年間（1567年-1572年）に築造されたものとしている。史料の記載によれば、明の隆慶年間に築造した中空式望楼は、1つあたりに総計4.5万の作業日を費やした。譚倫総督は明の皇帝への上奏文でこう述べたことがある。「今や、その（望楼のこと）規制が昔時とは完全に異なっているため、500人の労力が3ヵ月費やしても台座1つしか終わらせることが出来なかった」。長城築造労働者のほとんどは募集してきたもので、そのうち大工、石工、鉄工、左官、ペンキ屋、絵師、レンガづくりなどを含んでいるが、主力としてはやはり軍中の兵卒である。(P22-P26)

No.2 East Watchtower

Many watchtowers built in the Ming Dynasty are seriously damaged, and some remained walls are even on the verge of collapse. This watchtower is supported with wooden pillars and beams, which have now become rotten. However, the mirror-shaped stone pillar stands and hollows on the wall are well preserved. Legends has that this tower was in the original form of hollow watchtower designed by General Qi Jiguang. Solid and practical, hollow watchtowers were used to store weapons and dispose troops, and they could also used to transfer messages in battles, greatly improve the defense function of the Great Wall.

Besides the No.2 East Watchtower, there are also another seven watchtowers supported with wooden pillars and beams along the Simatai section, most of which stand on the western section. Experts estimate that watchtowers of such structure were built during the reign of Emperor Longqing (1567-1572) of the Ming Dynasty. According to historical records, each such watchtower built during the reign of Emperor Longqing needed a laborer to work for 450,000 days. Governor Tan Lun submitted a memorial to the emperor, in which he said that "the size [of watchtowers] today is different from those in the past and it cost three months for 500 laborers to complete a watchtower, so 50 tael of silver appreciated by the government to each tower is not enough to afford expenditure of recruiting artisans." This also proves that most workers at the time to construct the Great Wall were recruited. Among them include carpenters, stonemasons, kiln artisans, ironsmiths, plasterers, decorators and even painters, who had a specific division of labor. Yet army men made up the most crucial part of those laborers. (P22-P26)

동2루(東二樓)

명대 장성의 망루중에서 제일 심하게 훼손되어 잔존 부분의 벽체가 곧 무너질 것만 같은 부분이 있다. 이 망루의 서까래와 기둥은 나무구조로 되어 재목이 부식되고 없지만 고경식(古鏡式) 기둥초석과 벽채에 남은 기둥흔적은 뚜렷히 남아있다. 전하는 바에 의하면 이것은 척계광(戚繼光)이 창건한 공심적대(空心敵臺)의 최초 모양이라고 한다. 공심적대는 견고하고 실용적이어서 병사들이 투숙하고 병기를 저장하고 정보를 전달하며 전투시에 좌우로 호응할 수 있어 장성의 방어 능력을 최대한 크게 했다.

동이루 외에 사마대장성에는 서까래와 기둥이 나무구조로 된 망루가 7개 더 있는데 주로 장성 서단에 분포되어 있다. 전문가들의 추측에 따르면 이러한 구조의 망루는 명대 융경년간(1567년--1572년)에 건조되었다고 한다. 사료에 따르면 융경년간에 건조한 목조구조의 공심망루는 매 망루마다 노동력 약 4만 5,000 작업일을 사용했다고 한다. 총독 담륜(譚倫)이 황제에게 올린 상주문에는 "현재(망루)의 규제는 옛날과 달리 소요 인력 500명이 석달동안에 겨우 하나를 완공할 수 있으며" 조정에서 "망루에 배당하는 관록 은 50냥으로는 장인 고용비용으로도 부족하다"고 씌어 있다. 이는 당시 장성을 축조하는데 동원된 민부가 대부분 모집해 온 사람들이고 그중에는 목공·석공·벽돌공·도공·철공·미장공, 심지어 페인트공·화공 등이 있어 분담이 매우 세밀하였다. 하지만 주요 노동력은 여전히 군대들이었다.(P22-P26)

Ruine des östlichen Wachtturms Nr. 2

Sie befindet sich am westlichen Mauerabschnitt von Simatai. Früher gehörte dieser Wachtturm zu den 8 hohlen Wachttürmen in Holzkonstruktion, die in der Longqing-Regierungsperiode (1567—1572) der Ming-Dynastie unter der Leitung von dem damaligen bekannten General Qi Jiguang gebaut wurden. Heute sieht man an der Wand dieser Wachtturmruine noch viele Löcher, wo sich früher Holzsäulen befanden.

Der historischen Überlieferung zufolge betrugen die Baukosten jedes solchen Wachtturms 50 Tael Silber und dauerte die Bauzeit gut 3 Monate. Für Bau jedes Wachtturms mussten 500 Menschen eingesetzt werden. An den Bauarbeiten nahmen neben Soldaten auch eingestellte Zivilpersonen wie Tischler, Steinmetzen, Maurer, Schmiede, Ziegelhersteller und –brenner sowie Ansteicher und Maler.(P22-P26)

La tour de guet N° 2 de l'Est

Les tours de guet de la Grande Muraille des Ming ont été gravement endommagées et les murs des parties subsistantes sont également au point de s'effondrer. La tour N° 2 de l'Est comportait des poutres et des piliers de bois. Bien que les bois ne subsistent plus pour cause de pourriture, les socles de pierre en forme de miroir ancien et les trous destinés à recevoir les bouts des rondins dans les murs restent visibles. On dit que c'était le plus ancien modèle des tours de guet creuses créées par le général Qi Jiguang. Caractérisée par sa solidité et sa fiabilité, la tour creuse pouvait être affectée à cantonner des troupes, à stocker des armes et à transmettre des messages et permettait le soutien mutuel entre les tours voisines dans le combat, perfectionnant dans la plus grande mesure la fonction de défense de la Grande Muraille.

Excepté la tour de guet N° 2 de l'Est, la Grande Muraille de Simatai possède encore sept autres du même genre, réparties essentiellement dans la partie ouest. Les spécialistes estiment que les tours de guet ayant une telle structure ont été construites sous le règne Longqing (1567 – 1572) des Ming. D'après les annales, la construction d'une tour de guet de ce genre avait besoin d'une main-d'œuvre totalisant 45 000 journées de travail. Dans son rapport adressé à l'empereur, le gouverneur général Tan Lun a écrit : "En trois mois, 500 ouvriers ne peuvent réaliser qu'une seule tour de guet d'après le dessein actuel. Cinquante taels d'argent affectés à la construction d'une tour de guet ne suffisent pas pour payer les artisans." Ces écritures indiquent que la plupart des artisans participant à la construction de la Grande Muraille ont été recrutés, y compris des charpentiers, des tailleurs de pierre, des artisans des fours à briques et à chaux, des forgerons, des maçons, des vernisseurs et des peintres. La division du travail était assez détaillée, mais les soldats représentaient toujours le contingent principal de la main-d'œuvre.(P22-P26)

残存在墙体上的柱洞清晰可见
Column holes remained on the wall.
城壁の上に残った柱の穴
성벽위에 남아 있는 기둥구멍이 뚝뚝히 보인다.
An der Wand sieht man heute noch Löcher, wo sich früher Holzsäulen befanden.
L'encoche de pilier subsistant dans le mur est encore visible de nos jours.
Resti della base su cui poggiavano le colonne delle mura
Señal de la columna en la pared

La Torre Dong'er

Le torri di guardia risalenti all'epoca Ming sono in un grave stato di degrado e le parti rimaste in piedi della Muraglia sono anch'esse diroccate e fragili. La struttura portante della Torre Dong'er fu realizzata con travi e colonne di legno andate distrutte, ma si notano ancora chiaramente le basi su cui poggiavano le colonne e, sulle mura in rovina, i fori in cui le travi erano incastrate. Si racconta che questa torre fu la prima con la copertura a volta, ad essere edificata da Qi Jiguang. La torre migliorava la funzione difensiva della Muraglia, e fungeva anche da dormitorio per i soldati, da magazzino per le armi, per i cereali e la legna, oltre a punto di trasmissione d'informazioni verso le torri circostanti. Sulla Grande Muraglia di Simatai vi sono altre 7 torri di guardia come questa, con la struttura principale in legno. La maggior parte di esse si trova nella parte occidentale della Muraglia. Secondo gli esperti, queste torri furono costruite nel periodo del regno dell'imperatore Longqing (1567-1572) della dinastia Ming. Secondo alcuni documenti storici le torri di guardia a volta, realizzate con travi e colonne di legno durante il periodo del regno dell'imperatore Longqing, necessitarono, ciascuna, di 45.000 giorni di lavoro. Nella presentazione del rapporto del generale Tan Lun all'imperatore si legge: "...Per costruire una torre di guardia, così come stabilito dalla corte imperiale, si devono impiegare 500 operai per tre mesi di lavoro. Il denaro proveniente dalla corte imperiale non è sufficiente per il pagamento dei lavoratori reclutati". Da questo rapporto sappiamo che fra la maggior parte degli operai reclutati vi erano falegnami, scalpellini, fabbricanti di mattoni, fabbri, muratori, imbianchini, pittori ed altri ancora, ma che, tuttavia, furono i soldati a completare la maggior parte del lavoro. (P22-P26)

Segunda atalaya del este

Esta edificación de la dinastía Ming está hecha principalmente de madera, por lo que no extraña su avanzado deterioro. Incluso los muros están a punto de caerse. Las maderas usadas en la estructura ya son historia y sólo quedan las bases de piedra para las columnas. Se especula que la estructura fue inventada por Qi Jiguang, famoso general de la dinastía Ming, y se caracteriza por su fortaleza y naturaleza práctica. Su interior puede servir para guardar armas y esconder soldados. Las atalayas de este tipo facilitan el traslado de informaciones y el apoyo a tiempo a las tropas, en una palabra, mejoraron en gran medida la función defensiva de la Gran Muralla.

Además de esta atalaya, hay otras siete similares en Simatai, principalmente en el trecho occidental de la sección. Los expertos estiman que fueron construidas durante el reinado del emperador Longqing (1567-1572). Según los registros históricos, en aquel entonces la construcción de cada atalaya de esta estructura requería de 45 mil jornadas laborales. En un informe ante el emperador, un funcionario afirmó: "El sistema de las atalayas ya es muy diferente del anterior. En tres meses, 500 trabajadores sólo concluyeron una." "Las 50 onzas de plata que me ha entregado la corte no son suficientes para pagar a los artesanos." Dichas aseveraciones demuestran el alto número de trabajadores contratados para la construcción de la Gran Muralla, incluidos carpinteros, pedreros, albañiles, herreros, e incluso pintores y dibujantes, pero la principal mano de obra provino de los soldados. (P22-P26)

空心敌楼上残存的木梁洞痕迹
Beam holes remained on hollow watchtowers.
空心敵楼に残った柱の穴の跡
공심망루위에 남아 있는 나무들보의 구멍 흔적
Überreste des Kongxin-Wachtturms
Vestiges de trous recevant les poutres en bois dans le mur de la Tour de guet creuse.
Le rovine di una torre di guardia dove si possono notare i fori in cui venivano incastrate le travi
Señal de las vigas

司马台鸳鸯湖
The Mandarin Duck Lake.
司馬台の鴛鴦湖
사마대 원앙호
Der Yuanyang-See (Mandarinente-See) bei Simatai
Lac des Canards mandarins.
Il lago dell'Anatra Selvatica di Simatai
Manantiales de Yuanyang

（左页）司马台东二楼
(Left page) The No.2 Watchtower on the eastern Simatai Great Wall.
司馬台の東二楼
（왼쪽 면) 사마대 동 2 루

关门

关门是游人徒步登城的必经之处，距停车场约一千多米。关门贯穿墙内外，是边墙两侧的通路。关门靠外口原来设有大门，以控制行人出入。司马台长城东西两段共设有关门四处，均建在临近驻有士兵的敌台附近。(P28-29)

Pass Entrance

Lying more than a kilometer away from the Parking Lot, the Pass Entrance is a must passage for pedestrians to climb the Great Wall. It penetrates through the wall, linking its two sides together. There was originally a huge gate used to control stream of people outside the Pass Entrance. Along the entire Simatai section are four such entrances, all constructed adjacent to watchtowers stationed with troops. (P28-P29)

関門

関門は、徒歩観光客が長城に上る時どうしても通らなければならないところで、駐車場までは約1KM離れ、城壁を貫通して両側の道路と連結するように出来ている。外側は、関門を通して出入りする人をコントロールするための門があった。司馬台長城の東西両段に開かれた4つの関門は、いずれも守備部隊が常住する望楼付近に建てられている。(P28-P29)

관 문

관문은 여행객들이 도보로 성곽에 오를 때 반드시 거치게 되는 곳으로 주차장에서 약 1km 가량 떨어져 있다. 관문은 성벽 안팎을 관통하므로 성벽 양측의 통로로 된다. 관문의 바깥 어귀에는 원래 대문이 설치되어 있어 행인들의 출입을 통제했었다. 사마대장성의 동서 양단에는 4개의 관문이 설치되어 있는데 모두 병사들이 주둔하는 망루부근에 자리해 있다.(P28-P29)

司马台关门
The Simatai Pass.
司馬台の関門
사마대관문
Guanmen (Passtor)
La porte d'entrée de la citadelle de Simatai.
La Porta della "Chiusura" di Simatai
Pasos de Guanmen

Guanmen

Guanmen (Passtor), etwa 1 km von dem Parkplatz entfernt, ist der Einggang zur Großen Mauer. An der Simatai-Mauer gibt es insgesamt 4 solche Tore. Sie liegen in der Nähe der Wachttürme, wo früher Soldaten stationiert waren.(P28-P29)

La porte de la passe

La porte de la passe qui est à 1 km du parking est le seul passage à suivre pour les visiteurs voulant monter sur la Grande Muraille de Simatai. Il s'agit d'une ouverture percée dans la muraille, donnant accès aux deux côtés intérieur et extérieur de la Grande Muraille. Au début, on a mis en place une porte sur le côté extérieur dans le tunnel pour contrôler l'entrée et la sortie des passants. La Grande Muraille de Simatai est munie de 4 ouvertures avec porte dans ses deux parties est et ouest, dont chacune était à proximité d'une tour de guet où cantonnait une troupe.(P28-P29)

La Porta Guanmen (che chiude)

Situata a circa 1 chilometro dal parcheggio, la Porta Guanmen è l'ingresso obbligatorio attraverso cui i visitatori possono accedere alla Muraglia. Questa porta si trova fra il muro interno e quello esterno e costituisce l'accesso da cui si diparte, in due direzioni opposte, la grande Muraglia. In passato, presso questa porta, vi era un ingresso che serviva a controllare il flusso dei passanti. Sui lati occidentale ed orientale della Grande Muraglia di Simatai si trovano quattro Porte Guanmen presso ogni torre di guardia in cui risiedevano i soldati.(P28-P29)

Pasos de Guanmen

Los pasos de Guanmen, que distan unos mil metros del estacionamiento, son los únicos accesos para los turistas, quienes suben a pie. Estos se refieren a los pasillos que atraviesan las murallas laterales por debajo. Antes, había puertas que permitían controlar el acceso de visitantes. Hay en total cuatro pasos en los trechos occidental y oriental de Simatai, todos instalados al lado de las atalayas, desde las cuales era posible vigilar los accesos.(P28-P29)

司马台关门一角
A corner of the Simatai Pass.
司馬台関門の一角
사마대관문의 일부
Ein Teil des Passtors
Un coin de la porte d'entrée de la citadelle de Simatai.
Un dettaglio della Porta della "Chiusura"
Una rincón de Guanmen

垛口砖（石）

垛口封顶砖（石）上有一个小洞，用来固定武器和树立军旗。明代时从外国引进了一种叫"拂郎机"的武器，拂郎机下面有个轴，把轴插在小洞里，可以转动作扇形射击。(P30-P33)

Battlement Bricks or Stones

Some bricks or stones on the top of battlements have holes used to fasten weapons or army flags. During the Ming Dynasty, the government introduced a weapon named "Fulangji" from abroad. With its axletree fixed in a hole, the weapon could turn and shoot within a range of sector.(P30-P33)

垛口（射撃穴）レンガ

射撃穴の上部レンガの上には、兵器を固定したり軍旗を立てたりするための小さな穴がある。明代には外国から導入し、「佛郎機」と呼ばれる兵器があった。底部に軸が仕組まれた兵器で、この軸をレンガの穴に差し入れれば、扇形射撃が可能になる。(P30-P33)

성가퀴벽돌

성가퀴 꼭대기의 벽돌위에는 하나의 작은 구멍이 나있는데 무기를 고정시키거나 군기를 세워두는 곳이다. 명대에 외국으로부터 수입한 '브랑지' 라고 하는 무기는 밑부분에 하나의 축이 있어 그 축을 이 작은 구멍에 삽입하면 무기를 부채형으로 돌리면서 사격할 수 있었다.(P30-P33)

Zinnenstein und –ziegel

In Simatai sieht man fast auf jedem Zinnenstein oder Zinnenziegel ein Loch, wo in der Ming-Zeit Armeefahnen oder vom Ausland eingeführte Schießwaffen befestigt wurden. (P30-P33)

Les briques (pierres) de créneau

Un trou percé dans une des briques de l'assise supérieure servait à fixer l'arme ou à planter l'étendard. Sous les Ming, on a introduit de l'étranger une arme, appelée "franchis". Quand on a mis le goujon de la partie inférieure du franchis dans le trou de la brique, celui-ci pouvait pivoter et permettait de tirer en éventail.(P30-P33)

La merlatura

Sui mattoni e sulle pietre della merlatura della Muraglia si trovano picoli fori che servivano a tenere le armi e le bandiere dell'esercito. Infilando nei fori la parte inferiore del *Folangji*, un tipo di arma militare importata dall'estero durante la dinastia Ming, si poteva sparare a ventaglio.(P30-P33)

Losas de piedras entre las almenas

Sobre las losas de piedras entre las almenas hay agujeros, que sirven para fijar las armas o banderas. En la dinastía Ming, se introdujo un arma avanzada, la cual se introducía en los huecos y permitían los tiros en forma de abanico.(P30-P33)

城墙上的佛郎机孔
The axletree holes for weapons named "Fulangji" on the wall.
城壁の上に残った「佛郎機」の穴
성벽위의'브랑지' 사격구멍
Schießscharten an der Mauer
Trou réservé au franchis dans la muraille.
Fori utilizzati per poggiare le armi (*Folangji*)
Agujero para fijar el arma

（右页）司马台东三楼
(Right page) The No.3 Watchtower on the eastern Simatai Great Wall.
（右頁）司馬台の東三楼
（오른쪽 면）사마대 동 3 루
Der östliche Wachtturm Nr. 3 (rechte Seite)
La tour de guet N° 3 de l'est de la Grande Muraille de Simatai (page droite).
Simatai: la Torre Dongsan sulla Grande Muraglia (a destra)
Tercera atalaya del este (Página der.)

城墙上的礌石孔
Holes dug on the Great Wall.
城壁の上の石の孔
성벽위의 돌구멍
An der Mauer gibt es viele solche Löcher,
durch die man früher mit Stein den Feind schlagen konnte.
Trou pour le lancement des blocs de pierre fait dans la muraille.
I fori nella pietra
Agujeros en la muralla

单边墙

Single-Side Wall

第四楼前方是不足百米的石砌单边墙。这道墙高约3米，墙上布置两排砖围砌的射孔。射孔内口上沿的盖砖长达57公分，是这段长城中发现尺寸最大的砖，它体现了明代烧造砖材的高超水平。

单边墙是司马台长城的又一建筑特点，以不同的形式分段呈现。在东十二楼以东有几十米的砖砌单边墙，东十五楼（仙女楼）至东十六楼（望京楼）还有约300米长城砖封顶（部分地段）的石砌单边墙，当地人称其为"天桥"。

明代在修筑司马台长城时，有意识地保留了各个时期的建筑形式。比如：明朝洪武年间修建的营城、成化年间修建的单边墙、嘉靖年间修建的障墙和附墙台、隆庆三年至万历中期修建的城墙及各种空心敌楼，等等。这使得后人有机会一睹当时的建筑风格，具有极高的历史研究价值和观赏价值。(P34-P39)

Upward the No.4 Watchtower at Simatai is a single-side stone wall that stretches for no more than 100 meters. The three-meter-tall wall is equipped with two rows of embrasures laid with bricks. Each brick laid on the upper inside of an embrasure is 57 centimeters in length, known as the biggest of its kind found in this section of the Great Wall. The brick implies the superb brick-firing technique during the Ming Dynasty.

Appearing in varied forms, these single-side walls scattered in different parts of the Great Wall display another architectural characteristic of the Simatai Great Wall. There is a single-side brick wall stretching for dozens of meters east to the No.12 East Watchtower. Also, there is a single-side stone wall, part of which has its top laid with bricks, stretching about 300 meters between the No.15 East Watchtower (also known as the Fairy Tower) and the No.16 East Watchtower (also known as the Beijing-Watching Tower). It is locally called the Heavenly Stairway.

司马台长城东四楼和单边墙
The No.4 Watchtower and Single-Side Wall on the eastern Simatai Great Wall.
司馬台長城の東四楼と片側城壁
사마대장성의 동 4 루와 단변성벽
Der östliche Wachtturm Nr. 4 und die einseitige Steinmauer
La tour de guet N° 4 de l'est de la Grande Muraille de Simatai et les murs simples.
La Torre Dongsi e il muro Danbian sulla Grande Muraglia di Simatai
Cuarta atalaya del este y el muro de solo un lado

（右页）单边墙
(Right page) A single-side wall.
（右頁）片側城壁
(오른쪽 면) 단변성벽
Die einseitige Steinmauer (rechte Seite)
Mur simple.
Muri Danbian (a destra)
Muralla con parapetos de solo un lado

When the Simatai section was constructed, architectural styles of different times of the Ming Dynasty were remained of purpose. For instance, the battalion fortress built during the reign of Emperor Hongwu, the single-side walls built during the reign of Emperor Chenghua, the defense walls and supplementary wall terraces constructed during the reign of Emperor Jiajing, the walls and hollow watchtowers constructed from the third year of the reign of Emperor Longqing to the middle reign of Emperor Wanli, etc. These structures with high value for historical research and sightseeing give a chance for today's people to learn about architectural styles at the time.(P34 P39)

単辺牆（片側城壁）

　4番目望楼の手前は長さ100M足らずの「単辺牆」城壁である。高さが約3Mで、上には2列の射撃穴が開かれてある。射撃穴の上部レンガは、長さは57CMに達し、この区間の長城では最大のものである。明代の優れたレンガ造りの技術を具現している。

　「単辺牆」城壁は司馬台長城のもう1つの建築特色で、様々な区間で様々な形式を以って造られている。東12楼東に長さ数10Mのものを除けば、東15楼（仙女楼）から東16楼（望京楼）の間には、また約300Mの石づくりの「単辺牆」城壁がある。土地の人々はこの区間を「天橋」と呼んでいる。

　明代では、司馬台長城を構築するに当たり、例えば明の洪武年間の営城、成化年間の「単辺牆」城壁、嘉靖年間の「障牆」と「附牆台」、隆慶三年から万暦中期までの「城牆」と各種中空望楼など各時期の建築様式を意識的に留めた。おかげで現代の人々は、当時の様々な建築風格を一見することが出来ているのである。きわめて高い研究の価値を持っている。(P34-P39)

단변성벽

　네번째 망루 앞에는 100m 미만의 돌을 쌓아 만든 단변성벽이 있다. 이 성벽의 높이는 약 3m, 위에는 두 줄의 벽돌로 둘러 쌓은 사격구멍이 설치되어 있다. 사격구멍의 안쪽에 막아놓은 벽돌의 길이는 57cm에 달하는데 이 구간 장성에서 발견된 최대 벽돌이다. 이는 명대의 뛰어난 벽돌 소재(燒制)수준을 보여준다.

　단변성벽은 사마대장성의 또 하나의 건축 특색으로서 다양한 형식의 구간으로 나뉘어져 있다. 동 12루의 동쪽에 벽돌로 쌓은 몇십 미터의 단변성벽이 있고 동 15루(선녀루)에서 동 16루(망경루)까지에도 300m 가량의 일부 구간이 지붕이 있는 단변석벽으로 되었는데 당지의 사람들은 그것을 "천교(天橋)"라고 했다.

　명대에 사마대장성을 수축한 사람들은 의식적으로 각 시기의 건축형식을 보류해 두었다. 명대 홍무년간에 축조한 영성(營城)· 성화년간에 축조한 단변성벽· 가경년간에 축조한 장벽(障牆)과 부장대(附牆臺)· 융경 3년에서 만력 중기까지 축조한 성벽과 각종 공심망루 등이 바로 그러하다. 이러한 것들은 후세 사람들이 당시의 건축풍격을 볼 수 있게 하므로 매우 높은 역사적 연구 가치와 관상가치를 지닌다.(P34-P39)

Danbianqiang

　Danbianqiang (einseitige Mauer) liegt vor dem Wachtturm Nr. 4. Sie ist etwa hundert m lang und 3 m breit. An der Außenseite der Mauer gibt es zwei Reihen von Schießscharten. Oben auf jeder Schießscharte sieht man einen 57 cm langen Mauerziegel, den bis heute in Simatai gefundenen längsten seiner Art.

　Danbianqiang ist eine architektonische Besonderheit der Großen Mauer bei Simatai. Sie wurde in verschiedenen Regierungsperioden der Ming-Dynastie gebaut. Heute gibt es hier noch mehrere Mauerabschnitte. Im Osten des Wachtturms Nr. 12 sieht man einen mehrere Dutzende m langen Mauerabschnitt. Zwischen dem 15. Wachtturm (auch Fee-Wachtturm) und 16. Wachtturm (auch Wangjing-Wachtturm) gibt es noch eine 300 m lange, oben mit Ziegeln bedeckte und außen mit Stein bekleitete Mauer, die von den örtlichen Einwohnern als „Himmelbrücke" bezeichnet wird.

　Darüber hinaus sieht man in Simatai noch Yingcheng (Kasernen) aus der Hongwu-Regierungsperiode, einseitige Mauer aus der Chenghua-Regierungsperiode, Sperrmauer aus der Jiajing-Regierungsperiode sowie Stadtmauer und hohle Wachttürme aus der Longqing- und Wanli-Regierungsperiode der Ming-Dynastie.(P34-P39)

Les murs simples

　Devant la tour de guet N° 4 est le mur simple en pierre de moins de 100 m de long. Dans ce mur de 3 m de haut, on a ouvert deux rangées de meurtrières maçonnés en briques. Les briques posées au-dessus des ouvertures du côté intérieur des meurtrières mesurent chacune 57 cm de long. Ce sont les plus grandes briques découvertes dans la Grande Muraille de Simatai, témoignant du haut niveau de fabrication des briques sous les Ming.

　La présence des murs simples sous différentes formes constitue une autre caractéristique architecturale de la Grande Muraille de Simatai. A l'est de la tour de guet N° 12 est un mur simple s'étirant sur plusieurs dizaines de mètres, tandis que le mur simple de pierre surmonté de briques entre les tours de guet N°s 15 et 16 de l'Est est d'une longueur de 300 m, connu sous le nom de "Passerelle".

　Lors de la construction de la Grande Muraille de Simatai sous les Ming, on a préservé à dessein les formes architecturales de différentes époques, telles que la cité de garnison construite sous le règne Hongwu, les murs simples bâtis sous le règne Chenghua, les murs de barrière et les terrasses sur les contreforts construits sous le règne Jiajing, les remparts et toutes sortes de tours de guet creuses bâtis de l'an 3 Longqing au milieu du règne Wanli, etc. Tout cela nous permet de connaître le style architectural de l'époque et a une valeur inestimable pour l'étude de l'histoire et l'appréciation de l'art de construction des Ming.(P34-P39)

Muri Danbian (unilaterali)

　Davanti alla quarta torre di guardia si trova un muro unico lungo 100 metri e alto 3 metri. Sulla superficie del muro in mattoni sono disposte due file di fori per armi da fuoco, coperti sulla parte superiore da mattoni. I mattoni, lunghi 57 centimetri, sono del formato più grande presente su questo tratto di Muraglia Ming, ciò sta a testimoniare il livello d'alta tecnologia raggiunto dalle fornaci durante la dinastia Ming.

　Questo muro costituisce un'altra delle particolarità architettoniche della Grande Muraglia di Simatai, e si presenta in diverse fogge lungo la Muraglia. I muri di questo tipo, edificati in mattoni si trovano ad est della Torre *Dong Shi'er* e fra le Torri *Dong Shiwu* (Torre della Fata) e Dong Shiliu (Torre d'osservazione su Beijing) hanno una lunghezza di 300 m, e vengono chiamati dalla gente del posto *"Tianqiao"*. Durante la costruzione della Grande Muraglia di Simatai, gli architetti della dinastia Ming utilizzarono lo stile architettonico di diversi periodi, per esempio, i muri *Ying* costruiti durante il regno dell'imperatore Hongwu della dinastia Ming, i muri *Danbian* edificati durante il regno dell'imperatore Chenghua, i muri di "ostacolo" e la terrazza di muri secondari costruiti durante il regno dell'imperatore Jiajing, i muri di cinta e vari tipi di torri di guardia edificati fra il terzo anno del regno dell'imperatore Longqing e il secondo periodo del regno dell'imperatore Wanli, ecc. Tutto ciò offre l'opportunità di far conoscere l'architettura delle epoche passate ai discendenti e costituisce materia d'incommensurabile valore sia per lo studio della storia che per il patrimonio artistico.(P34-P39)

Muralla con parapeto de un solo lado

Delante de la cuarta atalaya se extienden casi cien metros de muralla con parapetos de un solo lado. De unos 3 m de altura, estos parapetos poseen dos filas de agujeros de tiros. Las losas que se colocan por el borde superior de los agujeros miden 57 cm de largo, siendo las de mayor tamaño en el segmento de Simatai. Para construir las mismas se empleó una alta técnica de adobe ideada en la dinastía Ming.

Los parapetos deun solo lado son otra peculiaridad arquitectónica de Simatai y aparecen en varios trechos de la Gran Muralla. Al este de la duodécima atalaya hay decenas de metros de parapetos de ladrillos; Entre la decimoquinta (Torre de Hada) y la decimosexta (Torre de Mirador de Beijing) también hay el parapeto de 300m de largo, hecho de piedra y revestido de losas, bautizado por los lugareños como"Puente al Cielo".

Mucho tiempo se requirió para construir La Gran Muralla, donde se reúnen varios estilos arquitectónicos representativos de varios periodos dentro de la dinastía Ming. Por ejemplo, los parapetos de un lado pertenecen a la etapa Chenghua.(P34-P39)

单边墙墙上的射孔
Loopholes on a single-side wall.
片側城壁の射撃孔
단변성벽에 나있는 사격구멍
Schießscharten der einseitigen Steinmauer
Meurtrières dans un mur simple.
Sparatoie sui muri Danbian
Agujeros de tiro en el muro de solo un lado

东十二楼的单边墙
The single-side wall of the East No.12 Watchtower.
東十二楼の片側城壁
동 12 루의 단변성벽
Die einseitige Steinmauer des östliche Wachtturms Nr. 12
Murs simples près de la tour de guet N° 12 de l'est.
Muri Danbian sulla Torre Dongshiyi
Muro de solo un lado de la Atalaya Doce del Este

单边墙
A single-side wall.
片側城壁
단변성벽
Die einseitige Steinmauer
Mur simple.
Muri Danbian
Muro de solo un lado

（右页）从空中俯瞰司马台长城
(Right page) A bird's eye view of the Simatai
Great Wall.
（右頁）空から司馬台長城を俯瞰する
（오른쪽 면）공중에서 내려다 본 사마대장성
Die Große Mauer bei Simatai, von der Luft
gesehen (rechte Seite)
Vue aérienne de la Grande Muraille de Simatai
(page droite).
Veduta aerea dalla Grande Muraglia (a destra)
Vista panorámica de la Gran Murall
en Simatai (Página der.)

白 楼

　　"白楼"是司马台长城的第八楼，距停车场 2 千米。从远处看去，敌楼靠北侧坍塌的两角上，砌墙的白灰散连在一起，白花花一片，因此当地人称此楼为"白楼"。(P41-P43)

White Tower

　　The White Tower, also known as the No.8 Watchtower of the Simatai Great Wall, is two kilometers away from the Parking Lot. Looked from the distance, two collapsed corners on the north side of the watchtower disperse white lime and thus form an expanse of whiteness; hence locals call it the White Tower.(P41-P43)

白楼

　　白楼は司馬台長城の 8 番目の望楼であり、駐車場までは 2KM。白楼の名前は、北側に倒れている望楼両端の壁は真っ白に見えているところに因んで、土地の人々がつけたものである。(P41-P43)

바이루

　　"바이루(白樓)"는 사마대장성의 여덟번째 망루로서 주차장에서 2km 떨어져 있다. 멀리서 바라보면 망루가 북쪽의 무너진 양각에 의거해 있고 성벽을 쌓는데 사용된 흰석회가 한데 엉켜붙어 있어 하얗게 보이므로 당지 사람들은 이 망루를 "백루" 라고 부른다.(P41-P43)

Bailuo

　　„Bailou" ist der Wachtturm Nr. 8 auf der Simatai-Mauer. Da viele Mauerziegel an seiner nördlichen Seite schon abgefallen sind, sieht man dort nur weißen Mörtel. Daher nennt man ihn Bailou (Weißen Wachtturm).(P41-P43)

La tour de guet Blanche

　　Il s'agit de la tour de guet N° 8 de la Grande Muraille de Simatai, se trouvant à 2 km du parking. Quand on regarde de loin, on voit une parcelle toute blanche sur le côté nord de la tour effondrée, d'où son nom. En réalité, c'est la chaux utilisée lorsqu'on bâtissait les murs, qui s'est dispersée sur le sol.(P41-P43)

司马台长城东八楼（白楼）
The No.8 Watchtower (also called White Tower) on the eastern Simatai Great Wall.
司馬台長城の東八楼(白楼)
사마대장성 동 8 루(바이루)
Der östliche Wachtturm Nr. 8, auch der Weiße Wachtturm genannt
La tour de guet N° 8 (Blanche) de l'est de la Grande Muraille de Simatai.
La Torre Dongba (Torre Bianca) sulla Grande Muraglia di Simatai
Octava atalaya del este (Atalaya Blanca)

La Torre Bianca

　　La Torre Bianca è l'ottava torre di guardia sulla Grande Muraglia di Simatai, e dista due chilometri dal parcheggio. Guardando da lontano, sui due angoli della parte settentrionale della torre di guardia in rovina, si può notare della polvere bianca sulle mura per questo motivo la gente del luogo le ha dato il nome di "Torre Bianca".(P41-P43)

Atalaya Blanca

　　Se trata de la octava atalaya de Simatai, a 2 mil metros del estacionamiento. Su lado norte ya está arruinado, por lo que puede ver la argamasa usada en su construcción. Desde lejos, parece una edificación pintada de blanco, de ahí que se le bautizara como "Atalaya Blanca".(P41-P43)

残留在白楼墙上的子弹
Bullets remained on the wall of the White Tower.
白楼の壁に残った銃弾
바이루 벽에 남아 있는 탄알
Einschusslöcher an der Mauer
Balles restant dans les murs de la tour de guet Blanche.
Pallottole incastrate sui muri della Torra Bianca
Las balas en el muro de la Atalaya Blanca

司马台白楼内景
Inside the White Tower on the Simatai Great Wall.
司馬台白楼の内部風景
사마대 바이루내부
Innenansicht des Weißen Wachtturms
Une vue de l'intérieur de la tour de guet Blanche.
L'interno della Torra Bianca di Simatai
Interior de la Atalaya Blanca

文字砖

文字砖是司马台长城又一看点。"白楼"东侧城墙外墙面有一片文字砖，上面写着"万历五年石塘路造"；在司马台长城东西两段发现多处文字砖，上刻有"万历六年镇虏骑兵营"、"万历六年振武营右造"、"万历六年延绥营造"等字样，文字砖的呈现形式也不一样，有阳文、阴文、正文、反文；字体有楷书、宋书、隶书、行书等。据考证，文字砖是戚继光修边时期，为了方便考核将士们烧砖和修边质量而想出的办法，以此来明确责任。(P44—P47)

Bricks with Inscriptions

Bricks with inscriptions are what worthy visiting for tourists to Simatai. On the outside of the wall east to the White Tower are such bricks, which carry such inscriptions as "Constructed by Shitang Route in the Fifth Year of Emperor Wanli's Reign." On other inscribed bricks discovered at Simatai are carved such inscriptions as "Constructed by Zhenlu Cavalry Battalion in the Sixth Year of Emperor Wanli's Reign," "Constructed by Zhenwu Right Battalion in the Sixth Year of Emperor Wanli's Reign" and "Constructed by Yansui Battalion in the Sixth Year of Emperor Wanli's Reign." The inscriptions are carved in relief, intaglio, regular or reverse. Their letterforms include regular script, Song typeface, official script and running script. It is proven that inscribed bricks was designed by General Qi Jiguang to define responsibility of soldiers firing bricks when he supervised the construction of the defense work.(P44-P47)

文字レンガ

文字レンガは司馬台長城のもう1つの見ものである。「白楼」東側城壁の外側にはこのような文字レンガが沢山ある。上には「万暦五年石塘路営造」と書いてある。司馬台長城の東西両段にも多くの文字レンガが発見されている。上には「万暦六年鎮虏騎兵営造」、「万暦六年振武営右造」、「万暦六年延綏営造」などと書かれている。レンガの形は様々で、彫刻の仕方には陽刻、陰刻、正文、反文があり、書体としては楷書、宋書、隶書、行書などがある。考証によれば、文字レンガは戚継光が長城築造用レンガの品質を保証するために考え出したアイディアであるという。(P44-P47)

글자벽돌

글자벽돌은 사마대장성의 또 하나의 볼거리이다. '바이루' 동쪽 성벽의 바깥면에는 글자가 있는 벽돌이 가득한데 벽돌에는 '萬歷六年石塘路造' '萬歷六年振武營右造' · '萬歷六年延綏營造' 라는 글자들이 새겨져 있다. 이러한 글자들은 형태도 각이하여 양문 · 음문 · 정문 · 반문이 있고 글자체도 다양하여 해서 · 송서 · 예서 · 행서 등이 있다. 고증에 의하면 이러한 벽돌은 척계광이 이곳에서 장성을 수축할 때 장수들의 벽돌구이와 작업 품질을 검사하기 위해 고안해낸 방법으로 책임제를 명확히 할 수 있은 것이다. (P44-P47)

Mauerziegel mit chinesischen Inschriften

In der Nähe des „Weißen Wachtturmes" und am östlichen und am westlichen Mauerabschnitt gibt es viele Mauerziegel mit eingeschnitzten chinesischen Inschriften in der Normarschrift, der Song-Schrift, der vereinfachten Kanzlerschrift und der Konzeptschrift wie „Im 5. Jahr der Wali-Regierungsperiode von dem Shitang-Bataillon gebaut", „Im 6. Jahr der Wanli-Regierungsperiode von dem Zhenlu-Kavalleriebataillon gebaut", „Im 6. Jahr der Wali-Regierungsperiode von dem Zhenwu-Bataillon gebaut" und „Im 6. Jahr der Wanli-Regierungsperiode von dem Yansui-Bataillon gebaut". Durch diese Inschriften kann man wissen, wann diese Ziegel gebrannt wurden oder von welcher Truppeneinheit die Mauer gebaut wurde. (P44-P47)

Les briques tamponnées

Il s'agit des briques portant des caractères qui constituent une autre attraction de la Grande Muraille de Simatai. Sur la face externe de la Grande Muraille à l'est de la tour de guet Blanche, on voit des briques portant des caractères chinois, indiquant la date de fabrication de ces briques et la désignation de l'unité militaire chargée des travaux : "Fabriquée en l'an 5 du règne Wanli (des Ming) par le bataillon de Shitang". Dans les deux parties est et ouest de la Grande Muraille de Simatai ont été découvertes de nombreuses briques portant des inscriptions telles que "Fabriquée en l'an 6 du règne Wanli par le bataillon de cavalerie Zhenlu", "Fabriquée en l'an 6 du règne Wanli par le bataillon de la droite de Zhenwu" et "Fabriquée en l'an 6 du règne Wanli par le bataillon de Yansui". Ces inscriptions sont composées de caractères gravés en relief ou en creux, justes ou inverses, en écriture régulière, de style Song, de forme carrée et arrondie aux angles ou cursive. Les documents historiques révèlent que c'était Qi Jiguang qui inventa les briques tamponnées pour faciliter le contrôle de la qualité des briques et des murs bâtis par les soldats et l'établissement des responsabilités.(P44-P47)

Mattoni con iscrizioni

Sulla parte esterna dei muri di cinta, ad est della Torre Bianca, vi sono alcuni mattoni con iscrizioni su cui si legge: "Edificato da Shitanglu durante il regno dell'imperatore Wanli"; su alcuni mattoni ritrovati nella parte occidentale ed orientale della Grande Muraglia di Simatai si legge: "Battaglione di cavalleria Zhenlu, nel sesto anno del regno dell'imperatore Wanli", "Edificato dal battaglione Zhengwuyou, nel sesto anno del regno dell'imperatore Wanli", "Edificato dal battaglione Yansue nel sesto anno del regno dell'imperatore Wanli". Le forme dei mattoni con iscrizioni sono svariate ed anche i caratteri impiegati sono diversi: vi sono caratteri a rilievo, ad intaglio, grossi, sottili, ed in stili calligrafici di tipo regolare (*kaishu*), in corsivo (*xingshu*), di tipo Song (*Songshu*) e ufficiale (*lishu*). Secondo alcune fonti storiche, durante il periodo in cui Qi Jiguang condusse lavori di ristrutturazione della Muraglia, fu inaugurata la tradizione dei mattoni con iscrizioni per testare la qualità delle fornaci e per controllare la robustezza della fortificazione realizzata dai soldati.(P44-P47)

Losas con caracteres inscritos

Es otro atractivo del segmento. En el lado exterior de la muralla al este de la Atalaya Blanca, se ve una losa con caracteres inscritos "hechos en el quinto año del reinado de Wanli, en la provincia de Shitang". En Simatai se han encontrado muchas losas como ésta, con inscripciones parecidas. Las hay cóncavas, convexas y de distintos cuerpos de caligrafía china. Según los expertos, la idea se debió al general Qi Jiguang, con el fin de mejorar la calidad de las losas y aumentar el sentido de responsabilidad de los elaboradores. (P44-P47)

司马台长城文字砖
Bricks with inscriptions on the Simatai Great Wall.
司馬台長城の文字レンガ
사마대장성의 글자박이벽돌
Mauerziegel mit chinesischen Inschriften
Briques tamponnées de la Grande Muraille de Simatai.
Iscrizioni sulla Grande Muraglia di Simatai
Losas con caracteres inscritos

司马台长城文字砖和文字砖墙
Bricks with inscriptions on the Simatai Great Wall.
司馬台長城の文字レンガと文字レンガでできた城壁
사마대장성의 글자박이벽돌과 글자박이벽돌벽
Mauerziegel mit chinesischen Inschriften und Mauerabschnitt aus Ziegeln mit
eingeschnitzten chinesischen Inschriften
Briques tamponnées et muraille bâtie en briques tamponnées.
Mattoni con iscrizioni sulla Grande Muraglia di Simati
Muro de losas con caracteres inscritos

司马台长城东九、十楼
The East No.9 and No.10 Watchtowers on the Simatai Great Wall.
司馬台長城の東九楼と東十楼
사마대장성 동 9 루와 10 루
Die östlichen Wachttürme Nr. 9 und 10
Les tours de guets Nᵒˢ 9 et 10 de l'est.
Le torri Dongjiu e Dongshi sulla Grande Muraglia di Simatai
La Atalaya Nueve y la Diez del Este

东十楼内景
Inside the East No.10 Watchtower.
東十楼の内部風景
동 10 루내부
Innenansicht des östlichen Wachtturms Nr. 10
Intérieur de la tour de guet N° 10 de l'est.
L'interno della Torre Dongshi
Interior de la Atalaya Diez del Este

48

司马台长城秋色
The Simatai Great Wall in autumn.
司馬台長城の秋景色
사마대장성의 가을
Herbstlandschaft bei Simatai
La Grande Muraille de Simatai en automne.
La Grande Muraglia di Simatai in autunno
Paisaje otoñal de Simatai

十一楼

十一楼距停车场约2.5千米。这段长城是沿着山脊修筑的，出于防御需要，城墙和敌楼在这里绕了个弯。这里紧靠天池，林木茂盛，视野开阔，是春、秋歇脚观景的好地方。(P50-P51)

No.11 Watchtower

The No.11 Watchtower, situated 2.5 kilometers away from the Parking Lot, is constructed along the mountain range. For the sake of the needs of defense, the Great Wall turns the corner there. Adjacent to the Heavenly Pond, this place is densely forested and enjoys a wide field of vision. It is an ideal place for visitors to view landscapes in spring and autumn.(P50-P51)

十一楼

駐車場まで2.5KM離れた望楼である。山々の急斜面に沿って伸びていく長城の城壁は、防御の必要からこのあたりでカーブをして造られている。天池に近く、林木が生い茂り、視界も広いため、春秋の景色を楽しむ最適な場所である。(P50-P51)

11 루

11 루는 주차장에서 약 2.5km 떨어져 있다. 이 구간 장성은 산등성이를 따라 축조되었는데 방어의 수요에 인해 성벽과 망루가 이곳에서 굽이를 지었다. 이곳은 친지와 매우 가깝고 임목이 무성하고 시야가 탁 트이어 봄철이나 가을에 다리를 쉬우며 경치를 관상하기 좋은 곳이다. (P50-P51)

司马台长城望海楼（东十一楼）
The Sea-Watching Tower (East No.11 Watchtower) on the Simatai Great Wall.
司馬台長城の望海楼（東十一楼）
사마대장성 망강부(동 11 루)
Der Wanghai-Wachtturm (auch der östlichtliche Wachtturm Nr. 11 genannt)
La tour de guet Ayant vue sur la mer (N° 11 de l'est).
Simatai: la Torre d'osservazione sul mare (Torre Dongshiyi)
Torre de Mirador del Mar (Atalaya Once del Este)

Wachtturm Nr. 11

   Dieser Wachtturm mit seiner Mauer liegt auf einem L-förmigen Bergrücken, 2,5 km von dem Parkplatz entfernt. Von diesem Wachtturm aus hat man im Frühling und Herbst eine herrliche Aussicht auf die umliegende Landschaft. In seiner Umgebung sieht man dichte Wälder und auch die Tianchi-Quelle.(P50-P51)

La tour de guet N° 11

   La tour de guet N° 11 est à 2,5 km du Parking. A cet endroit, la Grande Muraille fait un détour en suivant la ligne des crêtes de la montagne pour rendre la défense plus rassurée. Tout proche du Bassin céleste, cet endroit recouvert d'une végétation abondante et offrant un large champ visuel est un lieu de rêve pour se détendre ou admirer lc beau paysage. (P50-P51)

La Torre Shiyi

   La Torre Shiyi dista 2,5 chilometri dal parcheggio. Costruita sulla cresta del monte per necessità di difesa, la Muraglia qui crea una curva nel punto di congiunzione con la torre di guardia.

   Grazie alla presenza del Lago Celeste, ai numerosi alberi ed all'ampio panorama, questo è il luogo ideale per una sosta di riposo in primavera ed estate.(P50-P51)

Atalaya Once

   La atalaya dista 2,5 km del estacionamiento y pertenece a un tramo de murallas que se construyó a lo largo de la cresta montañosa. Para acentuar sus fines defensivos, se colocó un ángulo a la muralla en el sitio del mirador. Cerca del Estanque del Cielo, la atalaya está rodeada de una densa floresta y un amplio campo de vista. En primavera y otoño es sitio ideal para descansar durante el recorrido.(P50-P51)

沿东十一楼往上的长城外侧，有一块独立的岩石，岩壁上有一个扁圆形的小岩洞，洞里是清凉的泉水，这就是当地人说的"天池"。天池的水旱天不减，涝天不增。当地人到此放羊、打柴，也都以天池水解渴。这样神奇的天池水源究竟在哪儿，它的来龙去脉怎样，尚需进一步研究。

Heavenly Pond

There is a massive rock outside the Great Wall above the No.11 East Watchtower. On the rock there is an elliptical grotto filled with cool water, which is called the Heavenly Pond by locals. No matter dry or rain season, the water amount in the Heavenly Pond remains unchanged. Local people who come here to graze sheep or gather firewood all drink water from the pond. Where the water of the Heavenly Pond comes from is still unknown and needs further investigation.

天池

東11楼から上に伸びていく城壁の外側には1つの巨石が単独で立っている。この巨石の岩壁には清水が湧いてくる小さな扁円形の穴がある。ここは土地の人々が呼んでいる天池である。天池の水は日照りにあっても降雨が多すぎても、増減したりすることはない。その源は今日に至っても謎のままである。

천지

동 11 루를 따라 올라가면 장성의 바깥쪽에 바위 하나가 홀로 서있는데 암벽에 납작하고 둥근 작은 구멍이 나있고 그 굴속에는 맑고 시원한 샘물이 있다. 예가 바로 당지 사람들이 말하는 "천지" 이다. 천지의 물은 가물에도 줄어들지 않고 장마에도 붇지 않는다. 당지의 주민들은 이곳에 와서 양을 방목하거나 땔 나무를 할 때 천지의 물로 갈증을 풀곤 한다. 이렇듯 신비로운 천지의 수원은 도태체 어디며 그 내력이 어떤지는 진일보 연구해야 할 바이다.

Tianchi

Tianchi ist eine Quelle an einem riesigen Felsen. Sie liegt an der Außenseite der Mauer nahe am Wachttrum Nr. 11. Ihre Durchflussmenge ist das ganze Jahr hindurch unverändert. Das Quellwasser schmeckt sehr süß und erfrischend, daher kommen viele örtliche Viehhirten und Bauern oft hierher, um mit dem Quellwasser den Durst zu stillen.

Le Bassin céleste

Au-delà de la tour de guet N° 11 de l'Est et à l'extérieur de la Grande Muraille s'élève un rocher solitaire abritant une caverne aplatie de laquelle jaillit l'eau claire et rafraîchissante. C'est le "Bassin céleste" dont les habitants locaux parlent souvent. Le niveau de l'eau ne baisse pas pendent les années de sécheresse ni ne monte par temps pluvieux. Les bergers et les bûcherons locaux y viennent se désaltérer en buvant de l'eau de ce bassin. Où est la source de ce bassin curieux reste un secret à tirer au clair.

Il Lago Celeste

Lungo il lato esterno della Grande Muraglia, nella parte alta della torre Dongshiyi, si trova una roccia. Sul dirupo si trova una piccola grotta di forma ovale nel cui interno scorre una sorgente d'acqua limpida, chiamata dagli abitanti del luogo il "Lago Celeste". La quantità d'acqua nella fonte non varia mai, sia che sia la stagione delle piogge sia che sia la stagione secca. I pastori ed i boscaioli che giungono qui trovano un po' di ristoro, bevono l'acqua del lago e si riposano dalle loro fatiche. Resta ancora da risolvere però il mistero sulla sorgente del lago.

Estanque del Cielo

En el lado exterior de la muralla que pasa por encima de la undécima atalaya reposa una roca aislada, en la cual hay una pequeña cueva en forma elíptica. Dentro el agua fresca brota de la fuente bautizada por los lugareños como Estanque del Cielo. El agua no mengua en tiempo de sequía, ni aumenta con las lluvias, y abastece generalmente a los pastores de cabras y los leñadores. Nadie ha respondido hasta hoy de dónde proviene esta fuente mágica.

将军楼

将军楼是司马台长城的东十二楼，又称"五眼楼"，距停车场约3千米，它是司马台长城中建筑最精美的一座敌楼。这里视野开阔，地势险要，相传是明代将军指挥布防的场所，同时也是与司马台城堡信息传递的重要联络点。将军楼的做工非常讲究，下部条石合缝，上部磨砖到顶；内部用砖砌成两道大拱，三条通道，十个券门；中心室顶为八角藻井，置身其中，犹如步入中军大帐，威严之感油然而生。贴近箭窗的地方砌有横向小筒拱，其作用类似现在的窗帘槽，做工很考究；楼门的石柱上还雕刻着两朵并蒂西蕃莲花，连上端四周的砖檐也是五层砖的双层棱角檐。顶部望亭是整个将军楼中规模最大，做工最精细的一座。这座敌楼处处给人以精巧、细腻的感觉，仿佛它不是战争的防御设施，而是精雕细刻的一幢豪宅。(P53-P58)

General's Tower

The General's Tower, also called Five-Window Tower, is the No. 12 watchtower on the eastern part of the Simatai section of the Great Wall. Standing about three kilometers away from the Parking Lot, it is the most exquisite watchtower at Simatai. The tower enjoys a strategic location and a wide field of vision. Legend goes that it used to serve as a command post and an important liaison station to transfer messages to the Simatai Fortress during the Ming Dynasty. The tower features a superb craftsmanship. Its bottom is laid with stone blanks, and its top is built with polished bricks. In the tower are two arches, three passages and ten arched doors, all laid with bricks. The central chamber is decorated with an octagonal painted ceiling. Standing in the chamber, one may feel as if he were in an awful army tent. Close to the watching window is a transverse arched tube of exquisite craftsmanship, which is similar to today's curtain groove in function. The pillar of its gate is carved with twin lotus flowers, and the tower also has a stretching double-eave roof laid with five layers of bricks. The pavilion on the top is the largest and most exquisite one of its kind in the entire tower. With an exquisite and delicate touch, it seems as if the tower were not a defense work but an exquisitely-decorated, luxury residence.
 of exquisite craftsmanship, which is similar to today's curtain groove in function. The pillar of its gate is carved with twin lotus flowers, and the tower also has a stretching double-eave roof laid with five layers of bricks. The pavilion on the top is the largest and most exquisite one of its kind in the entire tower. With an exquisite and delicate touch, it seems as if the tower were not a defense work but an exquisitely-decorated, luxury residence. (P53-P58)

将軍楼

将軍楼とは司馬台長城の東12楼のことであり、またの名を「五眼楼」と称され、駐車場までは3KMで、司馬台長城の中でも建築が最も美しい望楼である。言い伝えでは、ここは明代の将軍が指揮所を置いたところで、作戦連絡と情報伝達の中

司马台长城将军楼（东十二楼）
The General Tower (East No.12 Watchtower) on the Simatai Great Wall.
司馬台長城の将軍楼（東十二楼）
사마대장성 장군루(동 12 루)
Der General-Wachtturm (auch der östliche Wachtturm Nr. 12 genannt)
La tour de guet du Général (N° 12 de l'est).
Simatai: la Torre del Generale (Torre Dongshi'er)
Torre del General (Atalaya Doce del Este)

地である。将軍楼は念入りに造られており、長い石を基礎とし、屋上までは黒レンガを用いた。内部はアーチ形天井を持つ3通路が開かれ、アーチ形門は10で、真ん中は八角形天井を持つ大部屋になっている。中に身をおけば、まるで軍中の指揮テントにでも入っているかのような錯覚をさせる。射撃窓に近いところには、横向きになっている小さな「筒拱」というのがあるが、今日のカーテンを掛ける仕組みに相当するもので、これも念入りに出来ている。楼門の石柱には2輪の蓮花が彫刻されており、上部は彫刻を施した2層からなる軒を頂いている。最上部の望亭は将軍楼全体でも最大規模で、最も精巧に造られた1つである。望楼全体は戦時の軍事防御施設というよりも、むしろ華麗な邸宅と言ってよい。(P53-P58)

장군루

　　장군루는 사마대장성의 동 12 루로서 "오안루(五眼楼)" 라고도 하며 주차장에서 약 3km 떨어져 있는데 사마대장성중에서 건축이 제일 아름다운 망루이다. 이곳은 시야가 탁 트이고 지세가 험요하여 명대에 장군이 방어를 지휘하던 장소였으며 또한 사마대성보에 정보를 전달하던 중요한 연락처였다고 한다. 장군루의 축조작업은 매우 엄밀하였다. 아래 부분은 길죽한 석재로 봉합하고 윗 부분은 꼭대기까지 벽돌을 다듬어 쌓았다. 내부는 벽돌로 두개의 아치형을 만들고 3 개의 통로를 내었으며 10 개의 권문을 세웠다. 중심실 천정은 팔각조정(藻井)으로 되어 있어 안에 들어서면 마치 중군(中軍)천막에 들어선듯 한 느낌이 든다. 화살창 가까이에는 작은 아치형 구멍이 가로 나있는데 그 역할은 현재의 커튼홈과 흡사한데 공예가 매우 정교하다. 망루문 석주에는 한쌍의 연꽃이 나란히 조각되어 있고 심지어 윗쪽 사이의 벽돌처마도 다섯층 벽돌중에서 두 층은 능형처마이다. 꼭대기부분의 망정(望亭)은 장군루에서 규모가 제일 크고 공예가 제일 섬세한 건물이다. 이 망루는 어디나 정교하고 섬세한 느낌을 주어 마치 전쟁의 방어시설이 아니라 정밀하게 조각해 만든 하나의 호화주택같다.(P53-P58)

„General-Wachtturm"

Der „General-Wachtturm", auch der östliche Wachtturm Nr. 12 und der Wuyan-Wachtturm" genannt, liegt 3 km von dem Parkplatz entfernt und ist der prächtigste der 35 Wachtürme bei Simatai. Die geografische Lage dieses Wachtturmes ist schwer zugänglich und strategisch sehr wichtig. Der Überlieferung zufolge diente er in der Ming-Zeit als Kommandostab und auch als wichtige Verbindungsstelle für die Nachrichtenübermittlung mit der Simatai-Burg. Der ganze Wachtturm, unten aus rechteckigen Steinplatten und oben aus Ziegeln gebaut, hat innen 2 Bogengänge, 3 Korridore und 10 bogenförmige Tore. Alle Torsäulen sind mit Lotosblumenmustern dekoriert. An den Dachvorsprüngen und an der Innenwand sieht man Reliefs von Tieren sowie Blumen- und Tiermuster. (P53-P58)

La tour de guet du Général

La tour de guet du Général est la douzième de l'Est de la Grande Muraille de Simatai, appelée aussi "tour à cinq ouvertures". Située à 3 km du Parking, elle est la plus belle tour de guet de la Grande Muraille de Simatai. Cet endroit offre un large champ visuel et constitue un point stratégique et difficile d'accès. On dit que c'était le lieu où les généraux des Ming mettaient des troupes en garnison et ordonnaient des opérations militaires et un point important du réseau de liaison pour transmettre des messages. La réalisation de cet ouvrage était très recherchée. Dans sa partie inférieure, les blocs de pierre rectangulaires ont rigoureusement été joints en un monobloc sur lequel repose le mur minutieusement bâti avec des briques bien positionnées. A l'intérieur, elle inclut deux grandes voûtes en briques, trois passages et dix portes voûtées. La pièce centrale a un plafond à caissons octogonaux. Quand on y est enté, on croyait qu'on était dans la grande tente du commandant où régnait une atmosphère inspirant la crainte. Du côté interne au-dessus des fenêtres sont de petites voûtes transversales qui jouent le rôle analogue à celui des coffrets à rideau. Sur les deux piliers de pierre flanquant la porte d'entrée sont sculptées des fleurs de passiflore jumelles. Même les auvents des quatre côtés de la tour ont été réalisés en 5 assises de briques dont celles de deux assises sont disposées en biais de façon à donner une dentelure au bord. Le pavillon d'observation reposant au centre du toit de la tour est le plus grand et le plus superbe par rapport aux autres. Ingénieusement conçus, minutieusement réalisée et richement décorée, la tour du Général donne l'impression qu'elle n'est pas un ouvrage de défense pendant la guerre, mais une somptueuse demeure.(P53-P58)

La Torre del Generale

La Torre del Generale è la dodicesima torre lungo il lato orientale della Grande Muraglia, chiamata anche "Torre con cinque aperture". Dista 3 chilometri dal parcheggio. Essa ha un'architettura raffinata ed elegante. Grazie alla sua posizione geografica d'importanza strategica, sull'alto di un pendio scosceso con un'ampia visuale, questa era la sede del comando generale ed anche il punto da cui avveniva lo scambio di comunicazioni con il castello di Simatai. La Torre del Generale fu realizzata con maestria e raffinatezza: nella parte bassa, la pavimentazione a lastre rettangolari è perfetta ed i mattoni nella parte superiore della torre sono lisci; all'interno si trovano due archi di grandi dimensioni realizzati in mattoni, tre ingressi e dieci porte ad arco; il soffitto della stanza centrale è a cassettoni di forma ottagonale. Sulle feritoie da cui venivano lanciate le frecce vi sono dei canali simili a quelli che oggi si usano per far scorrere le tende; sui due lati della porta d'ingresso sono scolpiti due fiori gemelli; la gronda del tetto fu realizzata a cinque livelli. Il padiglione di guardia, sul tetto della torre, è quello di dimensioni più grandi fra tutte le torri ed è quello che richiese maggior lavoro. Nell'osservare la Torre del Generale si ha la sensazione che non fosse solo una costruzione difensiva, ma piuttosto un'abitazione di lusso abbellita con decorazioni.(P53-P58)

Torre del General

La torre es la duodécima atalaya del este, denominada también como Torre de los Cinco Ojos, a 3 mil m del estacionamiento. Es la atalaya más hermosa y cuenta con un punto de observación clave y amplio campo de visión. Se dicen que fue la comandancia desde la cual los generales dirigían la defensa y al mismo tiempo punto de enlace para trasladar las informaciones. Toda la fortaleza está hecha de losas. En el interior hay dos arcos de ladrillo, tres pasillos y diez puertas de arcadas. En su sala central, el techo termina en una cúpula octogonal. En las ventanas hay dispositivos horizontales de delicada factura para colgar cortinas. Los motivos de flor de loto tallados en las columnas cerca de la puerta, el mirador labrado con mucho esmero, los dobles aleros de ladrillos, así como otros detalles de la obra, dotan a la fortaleza militar del lujo de una mansión.(P53-P58)

将军楼内的八角藻井
The octagonal painted ceiling of the General Tower.
将軍楼内の八角形天井「藻井」
장군루안의 팔각조정(藻井)

Die achteckige Kassettendecke des General-Wachtturms
Plafond à caissons octogonaux de la tour de guet du Général.
I cassettoni di forma ottagonale all'interno della Torre del Generale
Techo de la Torre del General

将军楼石门上的西蕃莲花石雕
The passionflower sculptures on the stone gate of the General Tower.
将軍楼石門の上の西蕃蓮花の石彫り
장군루 석문위의 서변연꽃 석조각
Das Steintor mit Lotosblumenmustern des General-Wachtturms
Fleurs de passiflore sculptées sur la porte de pierre de la tour de guet du Général.
Due fiori gemelli posti lateralmente, scolpiti sulla porta di pietra della Torre del Generale
Bajorrelieve en la puerta de la Torre del General

箭窗上砌有横向小拱券
A small arch above the loophole.
「箭窓」の上にできた横向の小さなアーチ形儲物格
화살창 위에 가로 놓인 작은 아치형 권무—시렁
Gewölbe eines Schießfensters
Petite voûte transversale au-dessus de la fenêtre de tir à l'arc.
Un piccolo arco orizzontale sopra la feritoia per le frecce
Ventanas con decoración

箭窗旁的储物格
A storage closet beside the loophole.
「箭窓」傍らの儲物格
화살창 옆에 있는 물품 보관 시렁
Nischen neben dem Schießfenster
Niches des deux côtés d'une fenêtre de tir à l'arc.
Una nicchia per conservare materiale presso la feritoia per le frecce
Estantes al lado de la ventana

将军楼内的砖砌大拱
A brick-laid arch inside the General Tower.
将軍楼内の大きなレンガ天井
장군루안의 벽돌로 쌓은 큰 아
치형 처마
Innenansicht des General-
Wachtturms
Grande voûte en briques dans la
tour de guet du Général.
Un grande arco di mattoni nella
Torre del Generale
Puerta en el interior de la Torre del
General

障墙

将军楼以东地势险要，南侧是悬崖峭壁，无法修筑普通的城墙。当年修长城时，劳动人民因地制宜，在山脊上用青砖修筑了这道特殊的长城，人们习惯上称它为"障墙"。障墙箭眼密布，形式多样，它居高临下，朝向低谷方向，用来防卫侵入边墙内侧敌人的进攻。障墙的军事价值在于作战时进可攻、退可守，步步为营。天梯上的障墙是最为壮观的，在20米的垂直落差内，从最顶上的障墙箭孔射箭，可以一直穿过所有障墙箭孔，到达最下的障墙，精巧程度令人赞叹不已。这种设计巧妙的建筑风格在所有长城中也是绝无仅有的。(P59-P63)

Defense Walls

The section east to the General's Tower features a dangerous topography. On both sides are perilous and deep valleys, so it is extremely hard to construct regular walls. For the sake of its geographic conditions, artisans built unique-styled walls with bricks on the mountain range, which are habitually called defense walls. On the walls are countless windows in various styles. Occupying a high position, the walls face a deep ravine and were used to defense the attack of enemy that invaded inside. A valuable military facility, the walls could be used to both attack and defense in wartime. Among the most magnificent are defense walls above the Heavenly Stairway. The walls have a vertical drop of 20 meters. It is astonishing that an arrow shot from an embrasure on the uppermost wall can directly go through that on the lowermost one. Moreover, their exquisite architectural style is unmatched among any other sections of the Great Wall. (P59-P63)

障牆（障害壁）

　　将軍楼以東は地形が険阻で、特に崖が切り立った南側は一般の城壁の築造ができないため、築造労働者は黒レンガを使った「障牆」を開発した。障牆は様々な形態のものがあり、射撃穴が密集し、来襲の敵を高いところから射撃できるように造られている。障牆の軍事価値は、主に攻撃の拠点としても、撤退時の拠点としても用いられるところにある。「天梯」区間の障牆は最も人々を驚嘆させている。垂直落差20Mの山の斜面に造られた幾つか障牆の一番上の射撃穴から矢を放せば、下のすべての障牆の射撃穴を通って、端末の障牆にある標的を命中できる。正確に設計して築造されたこのような建造物は、万里の長城の中においてもまれにしか見ないものである。(P59-P63)

장벽

　　장군루 동쪽은 지세가 험요하고 남쪽은 깎아지른 듯한 절벽이어서 일반적인 성벽을 축조하기 어렵게 되어 있다. 당시 이 장성을 축조할 때 역부들은 당지의 지형에 따라 산등성이에다 검은 벽돌로 이 특수한 성벽을 쌓았는데 사람들은 습관적으로 "장벽(障牆)"이라고 부른다. 장벽에는 화살구멍이 촘촘하고 형식이 다양하며 높은 곳에서 골짜기를 향해 내려다 볼 수 있으므로 적들의 진공을 쉽게 막을 수 있었다. 장벽의 군사적 가치는 작전시에 나아가 진공할 수도 있고 물러나 방어할 수도 있으며 진을 칠 수도 있는 것이다. 그중 천제(天梯)위의 장벽이 제일 장관을 이룬다. 20m의 수직 낙차내에 맨 꼭대기의 장벽에서 화살구멍으로 활을 쏘게 되면 화살이 곧바로 모든 장벽의 화살구멍을 통과하여 맨 아래의 장벽에 와 닿을 수 있는데 그 정밀도가 실로 사람들의 절찬을 자아낸다. 이처럼 교묘하게 설계된 건축풍격은 모든 장성가운데서 더는 찾아볼 수 없다.(P59-P63)

将军楼旁的瞭望台
A beacon beside the General Tower
将軍楼の一角にある望楼
장군루 옆에 있는 전망대
Beobachtungsstation neben dem
General-Wachtturm
Plate-forme d'observation à côté de
la tour de guet du Général.
La terrazza per osservare intorno
alla Torre del Generale
Punto de observación al lado de la
Torre del General

Sperrmauer

Die Sperrmauer ist ein Abschnitt der Tianti (Himmelsleiter) genannten Ziegelmauer mit zahlreichen Schießscharten. Sie befindet sich ganz oben auf einer steilen, 20 m hohen Felswand im Osten des „General-Wachtturmes" und ist daher sehr günstig sowohl für Angriff und auch für Verteidigung. Zum Beispiel konnte man damals mit Pfeilen von oben direkt nach unten auf eingedrungene Feinde schießen. (P59-P63)

Les murs de barrière

Le terrain à l'est de la tour de guet du Général est un point stratégique et difficile d'accès. Du côté sud, ce sont des falaises en surplomb et des précipices affreux où on n'a pu réaliser une Grande Muraille ordinaire. En tirant le meilleur parti du terrain, on a construit ce tronçon particulier en briques grises que l'on appelle habituellement "murs de barrière". Ces derniers sont percés de nombreuses meurtrières qui, de forme variée, occupant une position dominante et donnant sur les vallées, servaient à prévenir l'attaque de l'ennemi intrus à l'intérieur de la Grande Muraille. La valeur militaire des murs de barrière consiste en ce qu'ils permettent de déclencher l'offensive quand la troupe doit avancer, de se défendre lors du recul en prenant appui sur les fortifications denses. Le mur de barrière de l'Escalier menant au ciel est le plus spectaculaire. Sur une dénivellation de 20 m, une flèche tirée d'un trou percé dans le mur au niveau le plus élevé peut atteindre jusqu'au mur au niveau le plus bas à travers tous les trous sur sa trajectoire des différents murs. L'ingéniosité de la conception de ces murs est unique dans la construction de la Grande Muraille.(P59-P63)

I muri di "ostacolo"

Ad est della Torre del Generale, si trova un tratto della frontiera d'importanza strategica, a causa dei pendii troppo ripidi, non fu possibile costruire la Muraglia tradizionale, per cui in questo tratto fu eretto un muro che si inerpica sulla cresta del monte realizzato con mattoni grigi, chiamato muro di "ostacolo". Nella parte alta vi sono merli di svariate forme. Durante gli attacchi nemici aprire il fuoco dall'alto dei muri di "ostacolo"rendeva più facile il controllo della battaglia. Il valore militare di queste fortificazioni era quindi molto importante perché permetteva una migliore difesa. Il muro di "ostacolo" del *Tianti* è maestoso rispetto ad altre fortificazioni dello stesso genere. Costruiti lungo la cresta del monte, su un dislivello verticale di 20 metri, dai muri di "ostacolo" era possibile lanciare le freccie dai merli situati più in alto, e vederle oltrepassare tutti i merli fino a raggiungere quelli più in basso. L'architettura dei muri di "ostacolo" non è presente in nessun altro tratto della Grande Muraglia.(P59-P63)

Muros de Barreras

Al este de la Torre del General la configuración del terreno se hace más accidentada, mientras que al sur hay un precipicio. Esta condición no se permite levantar las murallas como en otros lugares, lo cual explica el porqué los trabajadores de épocas remotas levantaron varias filas de muros con las losas siguiendo la sinuosidad de la montaña. Las estructuras fueron denominadas Muros de Barreras. Los mismos están llenos de perforaciones para el tiro y se encuentran elevados y de frente al valle como defensa contra ataques enemigos que pudieran penetrar en el interior de la muralla. Los muros de la "Escalera al Cielo" son más impresionantes. Con 20 m de diferencia de nivel, los mismos permiten el paso hasta la base de una flecha lanzada desde la perforación de más arriba. Este diseño admirable no se encuentra en otro sitio de la Gran Muralla.(P59-P63)

障墙集射孔
Loopholes on the defense wall.
「障墻」の密集した射撃孔
장벽의 사격구멍
Schießscharten der Sperrmauer
Meurtrières serrées dans le mur de barrière.
Merli sui muri di difesa
Perforaciones en los Muros de Barreras

水边障墙
A defense wall on the riverside.
水際にできた「障墻」
물가의 장벽
Sperrmauer am Wasser
Murs de barrière au bord de l'eau.
Muro di difesa vicino all'acqua
Muros de Barreras al lado del lago

（右页）司马台长城东十三楼
(Right page) No.13 Watchtower on the eastern Simatai
Great Wall.
（右頁）司馬台長城の東十三楼
(오른쪽 면) 사마대장성 동 13 루
Der östliche Wachtturm Nr. 13 (rechte Seite)
La tour de guet N° 13 de l'est sur la Grande Muraille de
Simatai (page droite).
La Torre Dongshisan sulla Grande Muraglia di Simatai
(a destra)
Atalaya Trece del Este (Página der.)

天 梯

　　天梯距停车场3千米。远观天梯犹如翘起的大拇指，直指蓝天。这里的边墙异常险峻，宛如登天的梯子，由此得名"天梯"。天梯实际上是单面石砌的障墙，台阶随着山势步步升高，倾斜角度最大的地方有85度。

Heavenly Stairway

　　Situated three kilometers away from the Parking Lot, the Heavenly Stairway points upwards to the sky and looks from the distance like a stretched thumb. Extremely steep and perilous, the sidewall in this section looks like a stairway to the heaven, hence its name. Beside the sidewall is a stone stairway ascending along with the terrain, with the greatest obliquity of 85 degree.

天梯

　　駐車場まで3KM離れたところに所在し、遠くから見れば、まるで立った親指のようで、まっすぐ青空を指している。非常に険阻な所に造られた城壁は、立った梯のようであるところから名づけられた。城壁は、実のところ石で出来た片側城壁で、山の急斜面に沿って上へ伸びていく。山の勾配は最大85度に達している。

천제(天梯)

　　천제는 주차장에서 3km 떨어져 있다. 멀리서 바라보면 천제는 마치 쳐든 엄지손가락이 푸른 하늘을 가리키고 있는 듯 하다. 이곳 성벽은 매우 험준하여 하늘로 오르는 사다리같으므로 ' 천제' 라고 이름지었다. 천제는 사실 단면으로 돌을 쌓아올린 장벽으로서 층계가 산세를 따라 위로 뻗어 올랐으며 경사도가 제일 큰 곳은 85도에 달한다.

Tianti

　　Tianti ist ein Abschnitt der einseitigen Sperrmauer aus Stein und liegt 3 km von dem Parkplatz entfernt. Sie ist sehr steil. An der steilsten Stelle erreicht ihr Gefälle 85 Grad. Von weit gesehen sieht diese Steinmauer wie eine in den Himmel ragende Leiter aus, daher wird sie Tianti (Himmelsleiter) genannt.

L'Escalier menant au ciel

　　L'Escalier menant au ciel est à 3 km du Parking. Quand on le regarde de loin, il ressemble à un pouce dressé, pointant vers le ciel. A cet endroit, le rempart avec un faîte extrêmement raide évoque un escalier menant au ciel, d'où son nom. En fait, l'Escalier menant au ciel est un mur de barrière simple en pierre. L'escalier se prolonge vers le haut le long du versant de montagne extrêmement raide et à quelques endroits, l'inclinaison atteint jusqu'à 85°.

天梯和通天洞
The Heavenly Stairway and the Celestial Cave
天梯と通天洞
천제(天梯)와 통천동
Der Mauerabschnitt Tianti und die Tongtian-Höhle
L'Escalier menant au ciel et le Trou d'accès au ciel.
La scala *Tianti* e il foro verso il cielo
Escalera al Cielo

Tianti

Il *Tianti*, che dista 3 chilometri dal parcheggio, sembra un pollice che si alza verso il cielo. I muri laterali si arrampicano su pendii scoscesi, simili ad una scala che sale verso il cielo, da qui il nome di *Tianti*. In pratica il *Tianti* è un muro di "ostacolo". La rampa di scale al centro segue l'andamento della montagna verso l'alto. La pendenza delle mura arriva fino a 85 gradi.

Escalera al Cielo

Dista 3 mil del estacionamiento. Desde lejos semeja un pulgar que señala al cielo. Aquí los muros de barreras se alzan verticalmente, a guisa de escalera. El mayor ángulo de inclinación entre la escalera y el suelo llega a 85 grados.

司马台长城天梯
The Heavenly Stairway on the Simatai Great Wall.
司馬台長城の天梯
사마대장성의 천제
Der Mauerabschnitt Tianti
L'Escalier menant au ciel de la Grande Muraille de Simatai.
Una scala *Tianti* sulla Grande Muraglia
Escalera al Cielo de Simatai

天桥

　　仙女楼与望京楼遥遥相望，中间是弯曲交错的单边石砌墙，人称"天桥"。天桥两侧是刀削般的深壑，从上俯视令人心惊胆战。天桥的石墙上设有垛口，个别险要的地段，在低于石墙几十公分处有能容一脚的步道。跨越天桥，一定要小心谨慎。在天桥上还有一处险地叫"老虎嘴"，过老虎嘴时，身体要贴紧石壁，用手死死抠住石缝，一点一点地向前挪动，可谓险中之险。(P69—P71)

Heavenly Bridge

　　The wandering stone sidewall between the Fairy Tower and the Capital-Watching Tower is popularly called the Heavenly Bridge. On the sides of the walkway are deep valleys, and one may be captured by a feeling of horror if he looks downwards. In the most dangerous part, the walkway dozens of centimeters below the sidewall is so narrow that it allows only a single foot to walk through. Therefore, tourists must be careful when walking through the Heavenly Bridge. Another dangerous part there is called Tiger's Mouth. Passing this part, one had to move his feet slowly and gingerly while pressing his body as close to the cliff as possible and grasping the crevices on the wall at full tilt with fingers.(P69-P71)

天橋

　　遥かに相望んでいる仙女楼と望京楼とを連結するには、片側城壁づくりの長城がある。高い山の上に出来ているため、人々はこれを天橋と呼んでいる。天橋の両側は切り立った崖になっており、上から見下ろせば汗を握らせてびくびくさせてくれる。城壁の上には射撃穴が開かれてあり、特に険阻な区間の幅は、1人の人間がやっと通り過ぎれるような広さしかない。天橋を通り過ぎるのには要用心！天橋区間には「老虎嘴」と呼ばれるもう1ヵ所の難所がある。通り過ぎる時は、体を岩壁に貼り込め、岩の裂け目をしっかり掴んで用心深く進めなければならない。(P69-P71)

천교(天橋)

　　선녀루와 망경루는 멀리서 서로 바라보고 있는데 그 중간에 구불구불 서로 교차되는 단변석벽이 있으므로 사람들은 그것을 '천교'라고 부른다. 천교의 양켠은 칼로 베놓은 듯한 깊은 골짜기어서 위에서 아래를 내려다 보면 간담이 서늘해진다. 천교의 석벽에는 성가퀴가 없으며 개별적인 험요한 구간은 석벽보다 몇 십 cm 낮은 곳에 발로 겨우 디딜만큼한 길이 나있다. 천교를 지날 때는 반드시 조심해야 한다. 천교위에는 또 '주둥이' 라불리는 험요한 곳이 있는데 이곳을 지날 때는 몸을 석벽에 착 붙이고 손으로 돌틈을 단단히 잡으면서 한걸음 한걸음 움직여야 하므로 이른바 위험한 곳 중에서도 위험한 곳이다.(P69-P71)

Tianqiao

Tianqiao (Himmelsbrücke) ist ein Mauerabschnitt zwischen dem Xiannü- und dem Wangjing-Wachtturm. An beiden Seiten dieser einseitigen Steinmauer mit Zinnen sieht man tiefe Schluchten. Er ist ein schwer passierbarer Abschnitt. An manchen Stellen, zum Beispiel am „Tigermund", muss mann sehr vorsichtig sein und kann nur ganz langsam vorwärtskommen.(P69-P71)

La Passerelle

La tour de guet de la Fée et la tour de guet Ayant vue sur Beijing se regardent de loin, entre lesquelles s'étire en zigzag un mur simple de pierre, appelé "Passerelle". Des deux côtés de la Passerelle s'étendent deux ravins profonds aux escarpements à pic. Quand on regarde d'en haut vers le bas, on peut être pris de vertige. Le mur de la Passerelle est muni de créneaux. A certains endroits difficiles d'accès, à des dizaines de centimètres plus bas que le niveau du pied du mur, on a créé une piste d'une largeur ne permettant de poser qu'un seul pied. Il faut prendre beaucoup de précaution pour traverser la Passerelle. Sur la Passerelle, il existe un endroit constituant une barrière très difficile à franchir, connu sous le nom de "Gueule de tigre". Quand on passe par là, il faut être debout contre la paroi rocheuse, mettre les doigts dans la fissure entre les pierres et avancer tout doucement.(P69-P71)

Tianqiao

Fra la Torre della Fata e la Torre di osservazione su Beijing, si trova il tratto di muro serpeggiante noto col nome di *Tianqiao*. Lungo i due lati del *Tianqiao* vi sono dei ripidi burroni che precipitano come se il monte in quel punto fosse stato tagliato. I muri di pietra di *Tiaoqiao* hanno i bordi merlati. In alcune parti molto scoscese, per alcune centinaia di metri, vi sono stretti passaggi dove vi è appena lo spazio per appoggiare i piedi. Quando si scala il *Tianqiao* si deve fare molta attenzione. Nella parte alta del *Tianqiao* si trova un punto molto ripido chiamato "Bocca della Tigre". Quando si passa attraverso la Bocca della Tigre, ci si deve tenere stretti contro il muro, aggrapparsi saldamente alle fessure nella pietra e proseguire molto lentamente.(P69-P71)

Puente al Cielo

Entre la Torre de Hada y la del Mirador de Beijing, serpentea un tramo de parapetos de un solo lado, llamado "Puente al Cielo".A ambos lados del puente hay precipicios empinados, desde los cuales se marea el visitante cuando quiere mirar hacia abajo. Hay almenas en la pared, por debajo de la cual pasa un camino, a decenas de centímetros. En algunos sitios sólo hay espacio para poner un pie. Atravesar el Puente al Cielo requiere de mucha atención y cuidado. Al pasar la "Boca del Tigre", los exploradores deben pegarse a la pared del precipicio, meter los dedos en las fisuras de las rocas y avanzar poco a poco. (P69-P71)

仙女楼

离天梯顶端不远的山尖上有一座特别的敌楼，地基仅长5.6米，宽仅4.7米，它是司马台长城敌楼中身姿最为"苗条"的一座，当地人叫它"仙女楼"。"仙女楼"因建筑精美，汉白玉石券洞上刻有并蒂莲花浮雕而名气远播。仙女楼为两眼楼，高耸挺立，宛若仙女玉立于群山之巅，特别是雨后，云海茫茫，令人遐想，犹如来到仙境中的琼楼一般。而当银装素裹的冬季，银浪涛涛，仿佛天地相接，犹如进入了凝固的冰雪世界。(P72—P75)

Fairy Tower

There is a unique watchtower on the hilltop not far away from the top end of the Heavenly Stairway. Its foundation is only 5.6 meters long and 4.7 meters wide. As the most delicate one among watchtowers of the Simatai section, it is locally called the Fairy Tower. The watchtower is known far and near for its exquisite architecture, especially the stone sculptures of twin lotus flowers in its marble chamber. The Fairy Tower is a double-window watchtower and looks like a fairy standing amidst surrounding mountains. After the rain, in particular, the tower hidden in the sea of cloud has a fancy-arousing beauty, looking like a jade tower in the fairyland. In winter, the tower is coated with white snow. It seems as if the sky and the earth join together in the vast expanse of whiteness, and visitors seems to enter a stock-still world of ice and snow.(P72-P75)

仙女楼

　「天橋」までそんなに遠くないところに、基礎部の長さわずか 5.6M しかなく、幅わずか 4.7M しかない望楼がある。司馬台長城の望楼においてもとくに「痩せている」ため、土地の人々はこれを仙女楼と呼んでいる。造形が美しく、特にその漢白玉石づくりのアーチ形門の上に刻された蓮花は、名が広く知れ渡っている。仙女楼は 2 つの見張穴を設けた望楼で、山の頂に高く聳え立ち、遠くから見ればまるで天上界の美人のようで美しい。周辺の景色はすばらしく、特に雨や雪の日の、波を打つような山々の美しい景色は仙境そのものである。(P72-P75)

선녀루

　천제 꼭대기에서 멀지 않은 산정에 특별한 망루 하나가 있는데 기초의 길이가 5.6m, 너비가 4.7m 밖에 안되어 사마대장성의 망루중에서 제일 '가냘픈' 것이므로 당지의 사람들은 '선녀루' 라고 한다. '선녀루'는 건물이 정교하고 한백옥 석권동 위에 한쌍의 연꽃이 양각되어 있어 이름이 널리 알려져 있다. 선녀루는 양안루(兩眼樓)로서 거연히 솟은 모습이 마치 선녀가 뭇산의 정상에 서있는 듯 하다. 특히 비가 그친 뒤 구름이 망망할 때면 사람들로 하여금 마치 선경의 옥루에라도 온 듯 하고 만물이 소복 단장을 하는 겨울이 되면 은빛 파도가 하늘과 땅을 한데 이어놓아 마치 빙설세계에 들어선 듯 하다.(P72-P75)

Xiannülou

Es handelt sich dabei um einen nur 5,6 m langen und 4, 7 m breiten Wachtturm auf einer Bergspitze in der Nähe der „Himmelsleiter". Oben auf dem Bogentor aus weißem Marmor sieht man Reliefs von Lotosblumen. Von weit gesehen sieht dieser Wachtturm wie ein schönes Mädchen aus, daher wird er „Fee-Wachtturm" genannt. Die umliegende Landschaft ist im Sommer und auch im Winter besonders faszinierend.(P72-P75)

La tour de guet de la Fée

Non loin de l'extrémité de l'Escalier menant au ciel, à la cime d'une montagne s'élève une tour de guet très particulière. Occupant une surface de 5,6 m × 4,7 m, elle est la plus élancée des tours de guet de la Grande Muraille de Simatai. Les habitants locaux l'appellent "tour de la Fée". Elle est réputée pour les fleurs de lotus jumelles sculptées en relief sur le marbre blanc de sa voûte. Percée de deux ouvertures, elle évoque une fée qui domine de sa taille élancée et gracieuse les montagnes environnantes. Notamment après la pluie, on y assiste à une mer de nuages et on croit être dans la demeure magnifique du monde des immortels. Quand les montagnes étagées et dentelées sont couronnées de neige en hiver,

La Torre della Fata

Non lontano dal *Tianti* si trova una particolare torre di guardia le cui fondamenta sono di 5,6 metri di lunghezza e 4,7 metri di larghezza. Questa è chiamata la "Torre della Fata" ed è la più raffinata fra le torri di Simatai. È molto conosciuta per la bellezza della sua architettura. Sulla porta di marmo bianco è scolpita in rilievo una coppia di fiori di loto col gambo. La Torre della Fata ha due finestre. Dopo la pioggia la torre immersa nelle nuvole è simile all'immagine evanescente di un padiglione venuto fuori da un libro di favole. Durante la stagione invernale le dune argentate, si susseguono una dopo l'altra unendosi al cielo, ed improvvisamente il paesaggio prende forma come ghiaccio solidificato. (P72-P75)

Torre de Hada

Sobre la cima montañosa cerca del Puente al Cielo, se yergue una atalaya, con una base de 5,6 m de largo por 4,7 m de ancho. Se trata de la atalaya más "esbelta" entre todas, privilegiada por una hermosa estructura y minuciosos bajorrelieves de flor de loto en su puerta arqueada de mármol blanco. La atalaya de doble agujero, sobresale por encima de los picos a su alrededor, sobre todo en los días que siguen a la caída de lluvia o nieve. Su silueta suele recortarse contra el espeso mar de nubes, semejando un hada del mundo de los inmortales.(P72-P75)

望京楼

　　望京楼是司马台长城又一有名的敌楼，它高高耸立在海拔 986 米的老虎山的顶峰。该山峰是司马台（古北口）一线长城的最高点。远望望京楼就像一把锥子，直插蓝天，格外醒目，是摄影爱好者心中的圣地。据当地人讲，从前，当天晴日朗的时候，站在城楼上依稀可见北京的轮廓，夜晚可以望见北京的万家灯火，故得此名。但是，登望京楼绝非易事，要做劳筋骨出大汗的准备，而且，之前最好备足干粮饮水。望京楼距停车场约 4 千米。(P76-P85)

Beijing-Watching Tower

　　Another famous watchtower along the Simatai section, the Beijing-Watching Tower erects on the top of the Tiger Mountain that rises 986 meters above sea level. The mountain occupies the highest point along the Simatai-Gubeikou section of the Great Wall. From the distance, the eye-catching tower looks like an awl pointing upwards to the sky. It is a holy land in the hearts of photography lovers. On a sunny day in the past, locals said, people could see urban Beijing on the tower and lights emitted from tens of thousands of households at night, hence its name. But, it is not easy to climb onto the tower. Visitors must have enough preparation for sweating and exhausting work. Therefore, you'd better prepare enough water and food in advance. The tower is about four kilometers from the Parking Lot.(P76-P85)

望京楼

　　望京楼は司馬台長城のもう 1 つの望楼である。司馬台（古北口）一線長城の最高所で海抜 986M の老虎山上に聳え立っている。遠いところから見た望京楼は、まるで青空を指している錐のようで特に目立っている。土地の人々の話では、晴れた日にそこに上っていれば、昼間のなら北京市街の輪郭を、夜のなら北京市街の灯火が煌くようをかすかに見ることが出来る。望京楼が撮影愛好家の心の中のメッカではあるが、そこに上っていくことは決して容易なことではない。行く前は十分な携帯食品と飲み水を用意しておいたほうが一番いい。駐車場までは 4KM。(P76-P85)

망경루

　망경루(望京樓)는 사마대장성의 또 하나의 이름난 망루로서 해발 986m 의 노호산 꼭대기에 높이 솟아있다. 이 산봉은 사마대(고북구) 일선 장성의 감제고지이다. 멀리서 바라보면 마치 하나의 송곳마냥 푸른 하늘을 찌르고 있어 유달리 뚜렷하므로 촬영애호가들의 초점으로 된다. 당지인들의 말에 의하면 옛날에는 쾌청한 날이면 성루에서 멀리 베이징의 윤곽을 볼 수 있었고 밤이면 베이징의 야경을 볼 수 있어서 망경루라 부르게 되었다고 한다. 그러나 망경루에 오르기가 결코 쉬운 일이 아니어서 많은 땀과 힘을 들여야 할 뿐만 아니라 사전에 건량과 음료를 넉넉히 준비해야 한다. 망경루는 주차장에서 약 4km 떨어져 있다.(P76-P85)

Wanjinglou

　　Wangjinglou ist ein bekannter Wachtturm bei Simatai. Er liegt auf der Spitze des 986 m hohen Laohu-Berges, 4 km von dem Parkplatz entfernt. Der Laohu-Berg, auch Tiger-Berg genannt, ist der höchste Punkt der Großen Mauer bei Simatai und Gubeikou. Von diesem Wachtturm aus kann man bei gutem Wetter die Stadt Beijing erblicken. Er übt große Anziehungskraft auf Fotografen und auch auf Bergsteiger aus. (P76-P85)

La tour de guet Ayant vue sur Beijing

　　La tour de guet Ayant vue sur Beijing est une autre tour célèbre de la Grande Muraille de Simatai, dressée au sommet du mont du Tigre. Culminant à 986 m d'altitude, ce dernier est le mont le plus élevé le long de la Grande Muraille de Simatai (Gubeikou). Quand on regarde de loin cette tour, elle frappe le regard comme un poinçon pointant vers le ciel. Cet endroit est un lieu recherché pour les amateurs de photographie. D'après les habitants locaux, on peut apercevoir depuis cette tour le contour de la ville de Beijing par temps clair et une myriade de lumières scintillantes dans la ville pendant la nuit, ce qui lui vaut son nom. Pourtant, gagner la tour depuis le pied de la montagne n'est absolument pas une chose facile. Avant de partir, il faut préparer suffisamment de provisions et d'eau potable. La tour de guet Ayant vue sur Beijing est à 4 km du parking.(P76-P85)

（右页）望京楼和聚仙搂
(Right page) The Beijing-Watching Tower and Immortal Gathering Tower.
（右頁）望京楼と聚仙楼
（오른쪽 면）망경루와 취선루
Die Wachttürme Wangjing und Juxian (rechte Seite)
La tour de guet Ayant vue sur Beijing et la tour des Immortels (page droite)
La Torre d'osservazione su Beijing e la Torre del Raduno degli Immortali (a destra)
Torre del Mirador de Beijing y Torre de los Inmortales (Página der.)

La Torre *Wangjing* (di osservazione su Beijing)

La Torre *Wangjing* è un'altra torre molto famosa lungo la Grande Muraglia di Simatai. Si erige sulla cima del Monte della Tigre, ad un'altitudine di 986 metri sopra il livello del mare. Il monte della Tigre è il punto più elevato della Grande Muraglia di Simatai (Gubeikou). Da lontano, la Torre *Wangjing* sembra una lancia piantata nel cielo, questo è un luogo sacro per tutti i fotografi. In passato, nelle giornate di sole, dalla Torre *Wangjing* era possibile vedere i dintorni di Beijing, mentre di sera era possibile godere della veduta notturna della capitale. Tuttavia non è facile arrivare in cima alla torre; coloro che vorranno provare, dovranno portarsi da mangiare e da bere a sufficienza e, prepararsi a sudare non poco. La Torre *Wangjing* dista 4 chilometri dal parcheggio.(P76-P85)

Torre del Mirador de Beijing

La Torre del Mirador de Beijing es otra famosa atalaya de Simatai y se encuentra en la cima de la llamada Montaña del Tigre, a 986 m de altura sobre el nivel del mar. Es al mismo tiempo el punto más alto de la línea Simatai-Gubeikou de la Gran Muralla. De lejos, la torre parece a una lanza que apunta hacia el cielo y constituye tema favorito de los fotógrafos. Según se dice, en los días de buen tiempo, años atrás, se podía divisar toda la ciudad desde la torre, incluso de noche. Sin embargo, llegar a la misma supone mucho trabajo y para ellos se requieren suficientes víveres y agua. Dista unos 4 mil metros de la atalaya del estacionamiento.(P76-P85)

望京楼雪景
The Beijing-Watching Tower in snow.
望京楼の雪景色
망경루의 설경
Der Wangjing-Wachtturm nach dem Schneefall
La tour de guet Ayant vue sur Beijing après la neige.
La Torre d'osservazione su Beijing coperta di neve
La Torre del Mirador de Beijing después de nieve

司马台望京楼
The Beijing-Watching Tower on the Simatai Great Wall.
司馬台の望京楼
사마대 망경루
Der Wangjing-Wachtturm
La tour de guet Ayant vue sur Beijing.
Simatai: la Torre d'osservazione su Beijing
Torre del Mirador de Beijing

（左页）司马台望京楼东段残长城
(Left page) A collapsed section east to the Beijing-Watching Tower on the Simatai Great Wall.
（左頁）崩れた司馬台長城東段の望京楼城壁
（왼쪽 면）사마대 망경루구간 나머지장성
(Linke Seite)Überreste der Großen Mauer im Osten des Wangjing-Wachtturms
La section a l'est de la tour Ayant vue sur Beijing de la Grande Muraille de Simatai (page gauche).

La Torre di Guardia che volge verso Pechino situota lungo la sezione orientale della Grande Muraglia di Simatai. (a sinistra)
Partes arruinadas de la Gran Muralla al este de la Torre del Mirador de Beijing (Página izq.)

望京楼云海
The Beijing-Watching Tower in clouds.
望京楼と雲海
망경루의 구름바다
Der Wangjing-Wachttrum im Wolkenmeer
Mer de nuages enveloppant la tour de guet Ayant vue sur Beijing.
La Torre d'osservazione su Beijing avvolta dalle nuvole
Torre del Mirador de Beijing en el mar de nube

Da during the reign of Emperor Hongwu of the Ming Dynasty. It originally served as a command post of nearby stationed troops. With a rectangle layout, the fortress stretches 152 meters from east to west and 137 meters from north to south and covers an area of 20, 800 square meters. Its north and south gates have been both destroyed, only leaving two arched doorways. The bottom of the fortress walls is about 5.6 meters in thickness. The interior of the walls is covered with raw stone blanks, while the outside is laid with bricks. Some elderly locals recall that there were battlements on the top of the walls. There are two old roads retained respectively in the north and south of the fortress. The north and south gates connected by a south-to-north road do not directly face each other, but shift for about 30 meters. The west-to-east road deviates southwards from the fortress's west-east axis, and on the roadsides are preserved some old plain houses.

司马台城堡南门和影壁
The south gate and screen of the Simatai Fortress.
司馬台城堡南門と目隠し壁
사마대성보의 남문과 가림벽
Das Südtor der Simatai-Burg und die Abschirmungswand
La porte du Sud et le mur-écran de la citadelle de Simatai.
La porta meridionale del castello di Simatai e il "muro dell'ombra"
Paso austral de la Fortaleza de Simatai

사마대성보

사마대성보는 사마대장성에서 2km 떨어진 사마대촌에 자리해 있다. 기록에 따르면 사마대성보는 명대 홍무년간에 서달(徐達)이 건조한 것으로 원래는 주둔군 지휘소였다고 한다. 직사각형으로 된 사마대성보는 동서의 길이 152m, 남북의 너비 137m, 총 면적 2만 800㎡이다. 성보의 남북 두 문은 이미 훼손되고 아치형의 문길만 남아있을 뿐이다. 성벽은 기반 두께가 5.6m, 안쪽 처마는 큼직한 돌로 만들고 바깥 처마는 벽돌로 만들었다. 당지인들의 기억에 따르면 성보의 꼭대기에 원래는 성카퀴가 있었고 남북으로 통하는 두 갈래의 길도 오래된 것이었다. 남북향의 길은 성문을 마주하고 뻗었지만 두 성문은 결코 대칭되지 않고 동서로 약 30m 어긋나 있으며 동서향 길은 성보의 남쪽으로 치우쳐 있다. 도로의 양켠에는 아직도 옛 단층가옥들이 남아있다.

Simatai-Burg

Diese Burg befindet sich im Simatai-Dorf, 2 km von der Simatai-Mauer entfernt. Der historischen Überlieferung zufolge wurde sie in der Hongwu-Regierungsperiode der Ming-Dynastie unter Leitung des Generals Xu Da als Kommandostab der dort stationierten Truppen gebaut. Sie ist in ost-westlicher Richtung 152 m lang und in süd-nördlicher Richtung 137 m breit und nimmt eine Gesamtfläche von 20 800 Quadratmetern ein. An seinem südlichen und nördlichen Stadttor sieht man heute nur Überreste. Die 5,6 m breite Burgmauer ist aber noch gut erhalten. Früher gab es auf der Burgmauer Zinnen. Die ganze Burg ist durch zwei Hauptstraßen, eine süd-nördliche und eine ost-westliche Straße, in vier Teile eingeteilt. Heute gibt es an beiden Seiten dieser Straßen noch alte, ebenerdige Wohnhäuser.

La citadelle de Simatai

Les vestiges de la citadelle de Simatai sont dans le village du même nom à 2 km de la Grande Muraille de Simatai. Construite sous le règne Hongwu des Ming sous le patronage du général Xu Da, elle fut le siège du quartier général de la garnison. Ayant une forme rectangulaire, la citadelle mesure 152 m de long d'est en ouest sur 137 m de large du sud au nord, couvrant 20 800 m² de surface au total. Les deux portes d'entrée du sud et du nord ont déjà été détruites et il ne subsiste aujourd'hui que les voûtes des passages. Le pied de la muraille est de 5,6 m d'épaisseur. Le mur intérieur fut bâti avec des blocs de pierre, tandis que l'extérieur en briques. A l'origine, la muraille était surmontée d'un parapet crénelé. Maintenant, seul les anciennes allées du sud et du nord subsistent. Ces deux allées mènent respectivement à la porte du sud et à la porte du nord. Entre ces deux portes asymétriques, il y a 30 m d'écart d'est en ouest. L'allée disposée dans le sens d'est en ouest est moins éloignée de la muraille du sud que de celle du nord. Sur ses deux côtés, il subsiste encore des maisons sans étage anciennes et délabrées.

司马台城堡残城墙一角
A collapsed corner of the Simatai Fortress.
崩れた司馬台城堡の一角
사마대성보에 남아있는 성벽의 일부
Ruine der Simatai-Burg
Un coin délabré des murailles de la citadelle de Simatai.
Un angolo del castello di Simatai
Parte de la muralla arruinada de la Fortaleza de Simatai

Il Castello di Simatai

Il castello di Simatai è situato nel villaggio Simatai, a 2 chilometri dall'omonima Grande Muraglia. I documenti storici narrano che il castello, costruito da Xu Da durante il periodo del regno dell'imperatore Hongwu della dinastia Ming, fu la sede del comando dell'esercito stanziato in questa regione. Il castello, di forma rettangolare, lungo 152 metri da est a ovest, e 137 metri da nord a sud, copre una superficie complessiva di 20.800 metri quadrati. Le porte meridionale e settentrionale sono in stato di degrado, e si è conservato soltanto il passaggio della porta ad arco. Le fondamenta delle mura di cinta sono di 5,6 metri di spessore; il cornicione, nella parte interna è in pietra, mentre nella parte esterna è di mattoni. La struttura originaria del castello aveva i merli sul tetto. Due sentieri, uno a sud e l'altro a nord del castello, costituivano le vecchie vie d'accesso al castello. Il sentiero che va da sud verso nord è situato di fronte all'ingresso del castello. Le due porte del castello non sono simmetricamente opposte, ma ad una distanza di 30 metri l'una dall'altra. Il sentiero che va da est ad ovest si trova a sud del castello. Lungo il sentiero vi sono antiche abitazioni ad un piano unico.

司马台城堡北门及司马台村全景
The north gate of the Simatai Fortress and an overview of Simatai Village.
司馬台城堡北門と司馬台村全景
사마대성보의 북문 및 사마대촌 전경
Das Nordtor der Simatai-Burg und das gleichnamige Dorf
Panorama de la porte du Nord de la citadelle de Simatai et du village de Simatai.
La porta settentrionale del castello di Simatai e il panorama sul villaggio
Paso septentrional de la Fortaleza de Simatai y el poblado Simatai

Fortaleza de Simatai

Se ubica en el poblado de Simatai, a 2 mil metros de la Gran Muralla. Según registros históricos, fue construida por el general Xu Da los primeros años de la dinastía Ming y servía de sede a la comandancia. La fortaleza, de forma rectangular, ocupa 20,8 mil m² de superficie, de este a oeste mide 152m y de norte al sur, 137m. Las puertas se han deteriorado y sólo quedan los pasillos interiores que pasan por debajo de la muralla. Según los ancianos del lugar, hubo allí almenas que coronaban las murallas. Un antiguo camino zigzagueante conecta las puertas norte y sur, que no quedan una frente a otra en línea norte a sur, sino con un escalonamiento de 30 m. Otro camino de este a oeste pasa por el sur dentro de la fortaleza. A ambos lados se levantan aún casas de tiempos remotos.

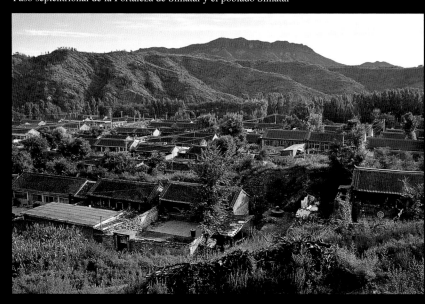

西线长城

　　西线长城较平缓，这里的观赏点很多，有完整的城墙、大量的文字砖群、富于变化的敌楼、捣米的石臼、麒麟影壁、障墙等等，而且，沿长城西行一直可以到达著名的金山岭长城。近几年，有很多团队选择这条旅游线路。这里还举行过多次长城穿越活动，如：万人徒步长城行、国际长城马拉松、穿越长城挑战自我、绿色环保行等。这些活动涉及面广，群众参与性强，深受中外游客的喜爱。

Western Section of the Great Wall

　　The western section of the Great Wall features a less obliquity. There are many scenic spots, such as intact walls, bricks with inscriptions, watchtowers in various styles, stone mortars to grind rice, unicorn screen and shield walls. Walking westwards, one may reach the famous Jinshanling section of the Great Wall. In recent years, this section has become a favorite itinerary among many travel groups. There have been held many events, including 10,000 People Walking Along the Great Wall, the International Marathon along the Great Wall, Challenging Myself by Walking Through the Great Wall and the Journey of Green and Environment Protection. All of these events have attracted many participants and are popular among tourists from both China and abroad.

西線長城

　　西線長城はわりあい緩やかで、一見の価値がある見ものとしては、完全に保たれた城壁、文字レンガ、変化に富んだ望楼、石臼、麒麟文様の目隠し壁などが挙げられる。城壁に沿って西へ行けば名高い金山嶺長城に到着できる。ここ数年、ここを狙う団体は増えている一方である。ここ数年ここで行われた長城をテーマとする一連の活動、たとえば「万人徒歩長城行」、「長城国際マラソン」、「長城を踏破して自らにチャレンジする」などの活動は、広く国内外の観光客から喜ばれている。

서쪽 코스 장성

　　서쪽 코스의 장성은 비교적 평탄하고 완만하며 볼만한 경관이 또한 매우 많다. 완전한 성벽·대량의 글자박이 벽돌·변화 많은 망루·쌀을 찧던 돌절구·기린가림벽·장벽 등이 있을 뿐만 아니라 장성을 따라 서쪽으로 곧추 나아가면 이름난 금산령장성에 이를 수 있다. 최근년간 많은 여행팀들이 이 관광코스를 선택하고 있다. 이곳에서는 또 1만명 도보장성여행·국제장성마라톤·장성통과자기도전·친환경장성관광 등 여러 차례의 장성통과행사가 거행되었다. 이러한 행사는 관련된 면이 넓고 대중성이 강하여 국내외 여행객들의 호평을 받고 있다.

麒麟影壁　　　　　　　　Die Abschirmungswand mit dem Muster des Fabeltiers *Qilin*
The Unicorn Screen.　　　 Mur-écran décoré d'une licorne sculptée.
「麒麟影壁」目隠し壁　　 Il "muro dell'ombra" Qilin
기린가림벽　　　　　　　Muro de Qilin

Der Westliche Abschnit der Simatai-Mauer

Dieser Mauerabschnitt ist heute noch gut erhalten. Das hiesige Gelände fällt kaum merklich ab. Hier gibt es viele Mauerziegel mit chinesischen Inschriften, verschiedenförmige Wachttürme, viele Kulturgegenstände, die in den letzten Jahren hier entdeckt wurden, wie Steinmörser und Steinstößel sowie die Abschirmungswand mit dem Muster von dem Fabeltier *Qilin* besichtigen. Von hier aus kann man westwärts die Große Mauer bei Jinshanling erreichen. In den letzten Jahren wurden hier verschiedene Veranstaltungen wie die Wanderung mit zehntausend Teilnehmern entlang der Großen Mauer, der internationale Marathonlauf entlang der Großen Mauer, die Propaganda-Reise für den Umweltschutz organisiert.

La partie ouest de la Grande Muraille de Simatai

La partie ouest de la Grande Muraille de Simatai est en pente relativement douce. Elle possède de nombreuses curiosités à voir telles que les murs bien préservés, les briques tamponnées, les tours de guet de forme variée, le mortier en pierre à décortiquer du riz, le mur-écran décoré d'une licorne sculptée, les murs de barrière, etc. Si l'on marche à pied vers l'ouest le long de la Grande Muraille, on peut arriver à la Grande Muraille de Jinshanling. Au cours de ces dernières années, beaucoup de groupes de touristes ont choisi ce circuit. A cet endroit, les activités de traversée de la Grande Muraille ont été organisées à maintes reprises et sous différentes formes, telles que la Marche à pied des dix mille personnes sur la Grande Muraille, le Marathon international sur la Grande Muraille, la Traversée de la Grande Muraille défiant soi-même, le Tour d'intérêt de la verdure et de la protection du milieu écologique, etc. Ayant les thèmes variés et avec une participation large, ces activités sont très prisées des touristes chinois et étrangers.

La Grande Muraglia che va verso ovest

La Grande Muraglia ad ovest è un tratto molto tranquillo, in cui sono presenti molti punti estremamente interessanti. È qui che si trovano mura ben conservate, un gran numero di mattoni con iscrizioni, torri di guardia dalle svariate fogge, il mortaio di pietra, lo schermo Qilin, i muri di "ostacolo" e molti altri elementi. Lungo la Grande Muraglia che si estende verso ovest si arriva a Jinshangling. Negli ultimi anni, molti gruppi turistici hanno percorso questo itinerario, qui si sono svolte molte manifestazioni come il "Viaggio a piedi sulla Grande Muraglia di diecimila visitatori", la "Maratona internazionale della Grande Muraglia",l' "Attraversamento della Grande Muraglia e la sfida con sé stessi", il "Viaggio verde della protezione ambientale" ed altre.

Gran Muralla en la línea occidental

Por el oeste de Simatai la Gran Muralla pasa por terrenos mucho más llanos y cuenta con muchos puntos de interés, como las murallas totalmente conservadas, las losas con inscripciones, las atalayas de diferentes formas, muros de barreras, etc. Además, siguiendo

esa línea se puede llegar a otro famoso tramo de la Gran Muralla – Jinshanling. En los últimos años muchos grupos de turistas han decidido emprender ese recorrido. Ha habido asimismo una serie de actividades y festejos en el lugar, como por ejemplo, la Caminata de Diez Mil Personas por la Gran Muralla y el Maratón Internacional de la Gran Muralla, de amplia repercusión social.

司马台西段长城
The western section of the Simatai Great Wall.
司馬台長城西段
사마대 서쪽 구간 장성
Der westlich Abschnitt der Großen Mauer bei Simatai.
La partie ouest de la Grande Muraille de Simatai.
La parte occidentale della Grande Muraglia di Simatai
Gran Muralla en la línea occidental de Simatai

司马台长城的西端与著名的金山岭长城相连。金山岭长城建于明洪武年间（1368年－1398年），由明朝著名将领谭伦和戚继光共同制定防御措施重新修建。这一段长城气势雄伟，视野开阔，构成了此段长城美与险的壮丽景象。

从金山岭长城再向西是万里长城的重要关口－古北口长城。

古北口长城位于北京密云县北部，主体长城将盘龙、卧虎二山连成一体。明洪武十一年（1378年）大将徐达重修了古北口长城，此段长城是通往北京的南北重要通道。

倫)과 척계광(戚繼光)이 공동으로 방어조치를 제정하여 새로 축조한 것이다. 이 구간 장성은 기세가 웅위롭고 시야가 탁 트이어 이 구간 장성의 미(美)와 험(險)의 장려한 경관을 구성하였다.

금산령장성에서 더 서쪽으로 나아가면 만리장성의 중요한 요도인 고북구(古北口)장성이 나진다.

고북구장성은 베이징 미윈(密雲)현 북부에 자리해 있으며 주체 장성은 반룡(盤龍)·와호(臥虎) 두 산을 한데 이어놓았다. 명대 홍무 11년(1378년)에 대장군 서달(徐達)이 고북구장성을 개축하였는데 이 구간 장성은 베이징으로 진출하는 중용한 통로이다.

Jinshanling and Gubeikou Great Wall

The Simatai Great Wall is connected to the famous Jinshanling Great Wall in the west. The Jinshanling section of the Great Wall, built during the reign of Emperor Hongwu (1368-1398) of the Ming Dynasty, was a defense work co-constructed by Tan Lun and Qi Jiguang, both eminent generals of the Ming Dynasty. This magnificent section offers a broad field of vision and combines beauty and danger.

To the west of the Jinshanling section is the Gubeikou Great Wall, an important passage along the entire Great Wall.

The Gubeikou Great Wall, situated in northern Miyun County, Beijing, links the Panlong Mountain to the Wohu Mountain. In 1378, the 11th year during the reign of Emperor Hongwu of the Ming Dynasty, General Xu Da rebuilt the Gubeikou Great Wall. This section is a significant passage to Beijing.

Die Große Mauer bei Jinshanling und Gubeikou

Die Große Mauer bei Simatai ist am Westen mit der Großen Mauer bei Jinshanling verbunden. Sie wurde in der Regierungsperiode (1368—1398) des Ming-Kaisers Hong Wu unter der Leitung der bekannten Generäle Tan Lun und Qi Jiguang gebaut. Dieser etwa zehn km lange Mauerabschnitt ist heute noch gut erhalten.

Von dem Jinshanling-Mauerabschnitt weiter westwärts kann man den Gubeikou-Mauerabschnitt erreichen.

Die Große Mauer bei Gubeikou liegt auf den Bergen Panlong und Wolong im Norden des Kreises Miyun der Stadt Beijing. Sie wurde im 11. Regierungsjahr (1378) des Ming-Kaisers Hong Wu unter der Leitung des Generals Xu Da erbaut und ist heute ebenfalls gut erhalten. Wegen seiner geografisch wichtigen Lage war diese Mauerabschnitt zu jener Zeit für den Verkehr zwichen dem Norden und Süden Beijings von großer Bedeutung.

金山嶺長城と古北口長城

司馬台長城は西端で著名な金山嶺長城と相連なっている。金山嶺長城は、明の洪武年間（1368年－1398年）、明代の著名な将領・戚継光が制定した防御措置に従って改築したものである。この区間の長城は、気勢が雄大で視野も広く、美と険とをそろえた美しい景色がある。

金山嶺長城から西へ行けば、万里の長城でも最も重要な関所－古北口長城に到着する。

古北口長城は北京市密雲県の北部にあり、主要城壁は臥竜と伏虎の2山を一体に連なっており、北から北京へ通じる大切な通路を守る狙いで、明の洪武十一年（1378年）、大将軍・徐達の主宰で改築したものである。

La Grande Muraille à Jinshanling et à Gubeikou

L'extrémité ouest de la Grande Muraille de Simatai est reliée à la célèbre Grande Muraille de Jinshanling. Cette dernière fut bâtie sous le règne Hongwu (1368 – 1398) de la dynastie des Ming et plus tard, elle fut reconstruite selon un projet de défense élaboré en commun par les fameux généraux Tan Lun et Qi Jiguang. Ce tronçon de la Grande Muraille est extrêmement majestueux et permet d'avoir un champ visuel large, apprécié surtout pour sa beauté et son accès difficile.

A l'ouest de la Grande Muraille de Jinshanling, c'est la Grande Muraille de Gubeikou, connue pour sa position d'importance stratégique.

Située dans la partie nord du district de Miyun, la Grande Muraille de Gubeikou relie le mont du Dragon lové et le mont du Tigre couché. En l'an 11 du règne Hongwu (1378) des Ming, la Grande Muraille de Gubeikou fut reconstruite sous le patronage du général Xu Da. Cette section de la Grande Muraille était un passage très important sur la grande voie nord-sud menant à Beijing.

La Grande Muraglia di Jinshanling e di Gubeikou

L'estremità occidentale della Grande Muraglia di Simatai si ricongiunge con la Grande Muraglia di Jinshanling. Costruita durante il regno dell'imperatore Hongwu (1368-1398) della dinastia Ming, dai famosi generali Tan Lun e Qi Jiguang, la maestosità di questa fortificazione ed il panorama a perdita d'occhio costituiscono il fascino principale di questo tratto di muraglia.

La Grande Muraglia di Gubeikou è il passo più importante della Grande Muraglia da Jinshanling verso ovest.

Gubeikou si trova nella parte settentrionale del distretto di Miyun. Questo tratto della Grande Muraglia si estende tra i monti Panlong e Wohu. Ricostruita dal generale Xu Da, nell'undicesimo anno del regno dell'imperatore Hongwu (1378) della dinastia Ming, il tratto della Grange Muraglia di Gubeikou è un passo strategico per l'accesso a Beijing da nord verso sud.

Sección de Jinshanling y de Gubeikou de la Gran Muralla

Al este de Simatai, continúa la sección de Jinshanling de la Gran Muralla. Este tramo se construyó durante el reinado del primer emperador de la dinastía Ming (1368-1398). Más tarde fue reconstruido por los famosos generales Tan Lun y Qi Jiguang. Aquí reina un aire majestuoso y los visitantes pueden disfrutar una vista panorámica, pletórica de belleza natural y dotada de una posición estratégica.

Más al este de Jinshanling, se sitúa un paso muy importante de la Gran Muralla, Gubeikou. Ubicada en el norte del distrito de Miyun de Beijing, la sección de Gubeikou fue construida en el año 1378 por el general Xu Da, que desbrozó camino entre dos colinas de la zona. El sitio sigue siendo núcleo de comunicación para Beijing.

古北口长城
The Gubeikou Great Wall.
古北口長城
고북구장성
Die Große Mauer bei Gubeikou
La Grande Muraille de Gubeikou.
La Grande Muraglia di Gubeikou
La sección Gubeikou de la Gran Muralla

司马台长城景区示意图

Sketch Map of Simatai Great Wall Scenic Area

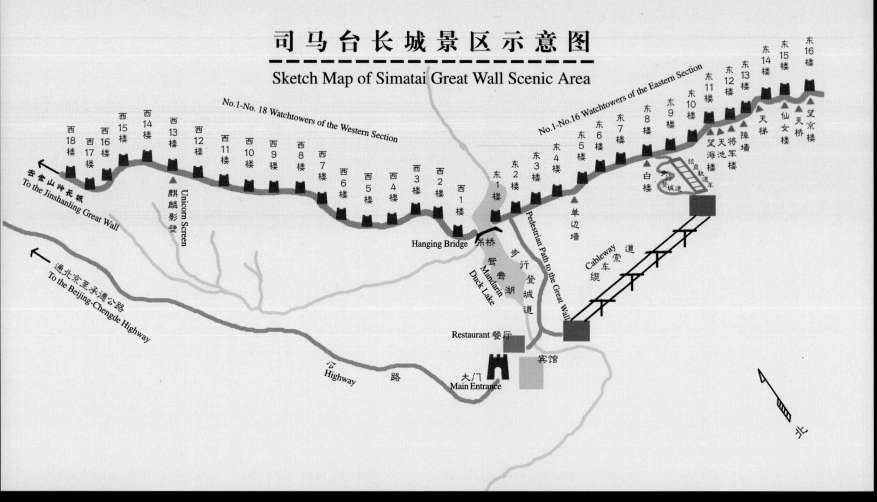

No.1-No. 18 Watchtowers of the Western Section

No.1-No.16 Watchtowers of the Eastern Section

东16楼
东15楼
东14楼
望京楼
仙女楼
天桥
天梯
东13楼
障墙
东12楼
将军楼
东11楼
天池
东10楼
望海楼
东9楼
东8楼
步行登城道
白楼
纹盘轨道车
东7楼
东6楼
东5楼
单边墙
东4楼
东3楼
东2楼
东1楼

西18楼
西17楼
西16楼
西15楼
西14楼
西13楼
西12楼
西11楼
西10楼
西9楼
西8楼
西7楼
西6楼
西5楼
西4楼
西3楼
西2楼
西1楼

麒麟影壁
Unicorn Screen

去金山岭长城
To the Jinshanling Great Wall

通北京至承德公路
To the Beijing-Chengde Highway

Hanging Bridge 吊桥

鸳鸯湖
Mandarin Duck Lake

步行登城道

Pedestrian Path to the Great Wall

Cableway 索道 缆车

公路 Highway

Restaurant 餐厅

宾馆

大门
Main Entrance

北

湖畔酒吧
Lakeside Bar.
湖畔バー
호숫가의 바
Eine am Seeufer
befindliche Bar
Bar au bord du lac.
Un bar lungo il lago
Bar al lado del lago

司马台石碑
The Simatai Stele.
司馬台石碑
사마대석비
Der Gedenkstein Simatai
La stèle de la Grande Muraille de Simatai.
Stele di pietra
Estela de piedra en Simatai

登城缆车索道
A cableway mounting to the Great Wall.
長城外国のケーブルカー
성상에 오르는 케이블카
Seilbahn bei Simatai
Téléphérique.
La funivia per arrivare alla Grande Muraglia di Simatai
Funicular en Simatai

"长城之最" 石碑
The stele carrying the inscriptions of "The utmost of the Great Wall."
石碑「長城のトップ」
"장성 제일"의 석비
Der Gedenkstein mit der Inschrift „Wunder der Großen Mauer"
Stèle des Records de la Grande Muraille.
La stele di pietra con l'iscrizione "La parte migliore della Grande Muraglia"
Estela de "Primero de la Gran Muralla"